THE
VOODOO WAVE

THE
VOODOO

W. W. NORTON & COMPANY   NEW YORK   LONDON

Mark Kreidler

Inside a Season of Triumph

and Tumult at Maverick's

WAVE

For information about permission to reproduce selections from this book,
write to Permissions, W. W. Norton & Company, Inc.,
500 Fifth Avenue, New York, NY 10110

For information about special discounts for bulk
purchases, please contact W. W. Norton Special Sales at
specialsales@wwnorton.com or 800-233-4830

Manufacturing by Courier Westford
Book design by Ellen Cipriano
Production manager: Devon Zahn

Library of Congress Cataloging-in-Publication Data

Kreidler, Mark.
The voodoo wave : inside a season of triumph
and tumult at Maverick's / Mark Kreidler. — 1st ed.
    p. cm.
ISBN 978-0-393-06535-0 (hardcover)
1. Surfing—California—Half Moon Bay.
2. Ocean waves—California—Half Moon Bay. I. Title.
GV839.65.C2K74 2011
797.320979469—dc23

                                        2011021770

W. W. Norton & Company, Inc.
500 Fifth Avenue, New York, N.Y. 10110
www.wwnorton.com

W. W. Norton & Company Ltd.
Castle House, 75/76 Wells Street, London W1T 3QT

1 2 3 4 5 6 7 8 9 0

*For my family
and for Donald and Shelly Wood
original soul surfers*

Mavericks—Half Moon Bay, California

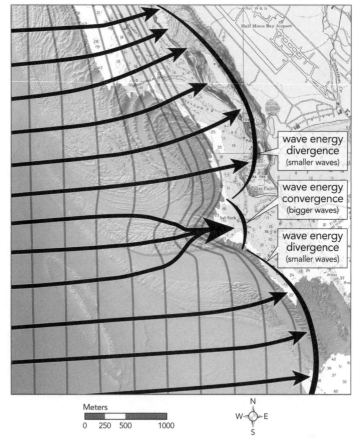

——— = wave crests   ➡ = wave "rays" or wave energy pathways

wave energy
divergence
(smaller waves)

wave energy
convergence
(bigger waves)

wave energy
divergence
(smaller waves)

Meters

0   250   500   1000

N
W–○–E
S

Wave energy is displaced up and down the coast around Half Moon Bay,
often the result of storms formed off the coast of Japan. The large arrow
in the center shows the point at which wave energies converge to form
Maverick's.

The reef came first. On the human scale, it has always been there. In geologic time, it was hundreds of thousands of years in the making—millions of years, maybe. And it was a fluke, the random result of a hodgepodge collection of rock and sand and sediment, thrust up and folded by the San Gregorio fault. As the years passed it became a fortress. While the beds around it withered and sank, the reef continued to thrive. In time it came to resemble nothing so much as a ramp, a fixed and dramatic rise in the ocean floor that could concentrate the deep, incessant swells of the Pacific Ocean and launch them heavenward. It gave birth to the wave.

Once people had found it, a half mile beyond little Pillar Point on the San Mateo County coastline in Northern California, they would imbue the surf point with human qualities: the wave was temperamental, or nasty, or benefi- cent, or treacherous. In reality, it was the most neutral thing in the world. It was a force, not a personality. The wave was relentless, and relentlessly changing. It stood at the far end of the storms that formed out over the North Pacific near Japan, storms that dragged wind across the water and created the friction that pushed the swells toward North America. When everything broke just right, when those swells came pulsing toward Half Moon Bay from the west at precisely the proper angle and with enough speed, and hit that reef-ramp more than 20 feet below the ocean's surface and stood straight up, they became curling mountains of water, hard and cold and— if you wanted to assign a personality trait to them—terribly unforgiving. The locals called it Maverick's.

Long before Jeff Clark made his first lonely journey to the outer reef in 1975, himself still just a teenager, Maverick's was there to be ridden. But not by many. To this day, it is among the most exclusive clubs in the world. While thousands of people over the years might eventually paddle out toward the break in order to say they've done it, or at least to see the wave up close, the truth is that perhaps 150 people on the planet have the constitution, skill, and basic disregard for personal safety to paddle in, stand up, and traverse the 40- or 50-foot wave faces under the forbidding conditions that the break routinely serves up. The water is frigid; the surf pattern can smash a rider almost directly into a jagged, exposed reef; great white sharks migrate through the area; the point is isolated and often cloaked in fog or deep gray cloud cover.

The payoff: the ride of a lifetime.

Before Clark was there, the reef stood formed; the wave was ready. It was a relentless force regardless of whether it was ever visited by man. Still, what Clark achieved in '75, all by himself, was a feat that becomes more lustrous year by year. He inaugurated a process that now brings the people from around the world to the point, to see it, to marvel at it, and, very occasionally, to attempt it. They come in groups, in the safety of numbers if they are surfers, and try to fathom the force before them. They think about Clark, exploring this world on his own, taking ultimate risks with no one trailing along to help him or initiate an emergency rescue, and they shake their heads. Sometimes they laugh out loud at the thought: such a crazy, reckless, inspired thing to do, daring fate that way. And they agree: you'd have to be out of your mind to try.

Chapter 1

ROUNDING THE CORNER AT PILLAR Point, the surfer faced the morning cloud cover and the light salt spray and emerged onto a thin strip of beach. The sandy runway led to the rocks and the seawall and, well beyond his sightline, massive green barrels of water that he knew were breaking out at sea. The storied ridge beside him already teemed with too many people for the bluff's crumbling edges to hold. And seeing the radical conditions around him and feeling the cold sand where he stood, and knowing what he knew, which only a lifetime spent at this precise point could tell him, Grant Washburn immediately understood two things.

First, he had an excellent chance either to catch the ride of his life or to get himself killed, with pain.

Second, the people on the water weren't the only ones about to get abused.

Standing there with his nine-foot eight-inch board in tow, Washburn, himself a towering six foot six, stopped momentarily to take in the scene unfolding around him. It was a circus on the sand. There were tents and booths everywhere, awards stands, scaffolding, sound equipment, sponsors' goodies piled on makeshift tables. There was a bourbon booth— were those mixed drinks being passed around? In the air, the festival aroma of pizza and sausages wafted through; vendors were peddling them a few yards away from a stand where you could buy your own Maverick's T-shirt and other memorabilia. It looked like the last hundred yards before the exit at a theme park.

From where the spectators were milling about, there was a zero percent chance of getting a decent look at the surf point itself and the wave that had brought about this carnival. All anyone could see were low clouds, high sun, and some water. They were better off buying a pepperoni slice and heading back home to watch the event webcast on their laptops. But Washburn already knew that the people here weren't going to leave. Most of them were rank amateurs; they didn't know what they didn't know. It was this thought, not the February air coming off the water from Maverick's, that sent a chill through Washburn.

Grant could tell at a glance that the spectators didn't understand that they would never be able to see the event from this vantage, not even if the clouds gave way to a perfect, crystalline afternoon. They had only the faintest idea that they were putting themselves in harm's way by standing so close to the seawall. And since it was a public area, no one was particularly motivated to tell them they shouldn't stand in a place where they had a legal right to be. Sure, you *could* stand there, but common sense and long experience told Grant that the spectators were almost guaranteed to get wave-whipped. But nothing was going to stop them today.

This was an event, after all. It was not a surf day, or at least not merely a surf day. The people in the water today were going to risk their lives and limbs to an extent that was unusual even by the rugged standards of this place; many of them were going to get trashed by the waves even if they avoided a full-blown tragedy. That idea alone made this a happening. Washburn had to admit the truth: even people who *did* know better—who knew the wave's fickle moods—were on the beach. There were results to be announced, a webcast to be produced, cell phone subscription plans to be hawked, an event to be recorded and edited, food to be sold.

Grant Washburn, at just that moment, felt that he was standing at the corner of Soul and Commerce avenues. It was right there at Pillar Point.

By that winter, Maverick's had by many accounts fulfilled its promoters' dream and become the Super Bowl of big-wave surfing events. It was classic overkill. However many people were too many, however much commercialism was too much, from now on the competition would approach the outer limits, then exceed them. Washburn had seen the event blossom and build for years on the commercial end; as one of the break's longtime veterans, he'd had a hand in the growing popularity of the place among people who had never surfed and would never surf. He had given innumerable interviews;

he had shared his time and knowledge with documentarians, surf scientists, feature writers, filmmakers. He had watched as the ensuing gold rush on the point nearly trampled one of his best friends, Jeff Clark, the founder of and godfather to the contest itself. Grant had surfed in every competition, filmed the wave dozens of times, and collaborated on a book of photos and surf essays about it. He was proud to be one of the tiny handful of humans who would ever attempt something as clearly insane as chasing down the side of a 50-foot wave face; and he believed in celebrating, not hiding, the fact of the site and of those who, like him, loved it without reservation.

Neither Washburn nor any of his brothers in competition opposed getting a little appearance money to surf the wave that they gleefully rode for free, or at a net loss, during the rest of the season. It was the time on the water that they all valued anyway, the fraternity and the challenge and the risk and thrill of it, and that indescribable reward of harnessing a tiny fraction of the awesome natural power that rolled and rumbled through Pillar Point, eternal and unrelenting. That part was spiritual and real. The rest was simply business—grabbing a little bit of the coin that other people had figured out how to wring out of Mavs. If anyone deserved a piece, surely it was the guys taking the chances.

Still, today was different. It was bigger and scarier in the water, more crowded and more disorganized on land. Washburn already could see ahead; he could see where it was going to go bad. He didn't want anybody in pain who hadn't volunteered for it. "You're going to get washed away," Washburn said matter-of-factly to the cluster of phone-company vendors in front of him. He looked around again and remembered why, years before, he had told his wife and daughters to stop coming to the beach on contest day. He alone among the Washburns would be the one to take chances—and even then, at age forty-two, the risks he was willing to take on the wave were more calculated than ever. Nevertheless, the risks were there, and they carried a heavy penalty—never more so than today. There would be no such rolls of the dice on behalf of the other Washburns.

Across the sand, Grant found some of the people who were trying to handle security and safety, and he told them to move the merchandise and the tents—and, most of all, the spectators—to a safer location behind the bluff. Washburn knew that water was going to come crashing through the skinny strip of beach, blasting jets of heavy spray over the seawall and swamping everything in its path. It felt like that kind of a day, and to a surfer, that feel was everything. In truth, to anyone who had spent time at Maverick's over the years, this was an automatic conclusion based on the conditions. Waves were forming so far out in the water and bearing down on Maverick's with such force that they were bound to carry remnants of that potent energy all the way into the seawall. It had happened thousands of times before.

Beyond that, what was about to occur had been right there on anyone's computer screen to see, and it had been there for a while. Washburn and the other surfers had seen these swells moving across the Pacific for days; they'd been tracking the storm from its inception, following the forecast models that their colleague Mark Sponsler had built on his website. This particular wave pattern had threaded the needle and made it across nearly 2,000 miles of open sea, all the way through to this one tiny dot on the map, and it was a beast. The surfers were stoked beyond all measure. Even for a storm that had created such giant swells, it was still an unbelievable long shot for all of the many variables to line up exactly right and deliver the big wave to Maverick's. It always seemed like a miracle when it happened.

This time, the surf was going to be epic. And epic out on the water meant a potential catastrophe on the beach.

Some part of Washburn wanted to find a megaphone and scream to the assembled masses to get out of danger, but he knew it would do little good. And ultimately Grant Washburn was here to surf, not handle security. His heat in the contest was going to begin soon. He wanted to get in the water and paddle out to really take a look at the waves that Mavs had produced for him today. He shook his head in dismay at the spectacle on the beach. He wasn't the world police—but maybe somebody needed to be. One of the security workers had nodded to Grant when he spoke of the danger, nodded as if to say he understood what Washburn was trying to tell him about moving everyone well away from the likely area of impact, but Grant felt sure that nothing was going to change. The sponsors were still arriving. The TV and webcast folks were dialed in. The fog was going to burn off into a spectacular, postcard-perfect afternoon, and the surfers were going to dance inside a watery maw for the amusement—and perhaps amazement—of the masses.

The fans wanted what they wanted. It was going to be a show.

Washburn took his board and moved away from the masses, into the shallows. Paddling out, he now could see the waves coming in, the sets lining up nearly a full mile out to sea. It was gargantuan. Grant could not stop what was coming; it was futile to try. What he could do was to make his way out there, as he had for the past fifteen years, and connect with it. It was not often this massive and this risky, and never on a contest day; but it was here. It was the real wave, and Grant Washburn knew exactly what to do about that part, at least. He knew how to embrace the energy, to align with the natural forces, to harness the adrenaline, steady the nerves, and take the ride. He knew that today everything could change, for better and for worse.

And Grant thought, too, about Mark Foo, a well known, big-riding Hawaiian surfer who years ago had died here on a wave that shouldn't have killed him, on a day that was nowhere near this huge. Foo's tragic passing stood as a cold reminder that any of the surfers could get themselves crushed by what might appear to be normal conditions. It was a part of the outsized risk to which they all were addicted. But today was beyond that. Today was one of those days—Grant knew it with barely a glance—on which all the training in the world, all the physical strength and stamina, was not going to get anyone through to the other side in one piece. You weren't going to survive it simply because you had lifted the most weights or done the most land exercise or practiced holding your breath the longest. It wasn't about fitness or bravado; it was not about strength. You could not will yourself past the danger. This time, Maverick's wanted a pound of your experience and four-score that of your respect. Anything less would get you clubbed.

A FEW HOURS EARLIER, before Washburn made his way to the water, his colleague, the Cape Towner, tossed and turned, trying for sleep. It was a rest that Chris Bertish desperately needed, even a couple of hours' worth. But he knew it was not going to happen, not yet. The vision kept failing. When the vision failed, there could be no peace.

Chris was a hopeful person by choice, but this problem had to be solved. It was not a matter of location; he did not feel lost. He wasn't frazzled. He was a little wired, predictably, after thirty-six consecutive hours of travel in which he had argued himself onto the last possible connecting flight to the West Coast, lost all his gear somewhere in transit, and then found himself trying to dial it down while crashing at someone else's place. But none of that, of itself, was necessarily unique; Chris had experienced most of it in some form or other dozens of times. After all, globetrotting on short notice had its challenges. He knew from experience that when he finally gave in, allowed himself to complete the image inside his head, he would be able to rest for a few hours. The problem was that he couldn't give in. He couldn't let it go. The scene kept coming out wrong.

Bertish had always visualized. It was how he mentally prepared to descend waves the size of buildings. Especially on the night before a big contest, Chris would go through the entire surf sequence in his mind's eye, dissecting the ins and outs of each wave until he could see his clear path from the lip down the face, through the curl, and out the other side. He would see himself paddling into position and dropping into the wave, stomping on his board with a powerful right foot and setting a solid rail in the churning water. The giant liquid barrel would thicken overhead, and Chris would find his way through, his timing perfect and pure. He would ride precisely as he wanted, in one clean stroke, and the wave would allow him to pass in peace. It was rhythmic and universal, the epitome of his connection with the ocean and with the wave.

The vision was beautiful and flowing. It also was comically out of line with what actually happened on the open water most of the time. Out there it was all churn and foam; it was noise like a freight train thundering through your skull. It was constantly heightened senses, and adrenaline absorbed by the pound. Chris was one of the authentic hard chargers in big-wave surfing. He took on gargantuan sets that other guys passed on, and his efforts were repaid in exhilaration and thrill—and also, sometimes, in pain, disorientation, exhaustion. Chris, from his teens on now into his mid-thirties, was constantly willing to throw himself into the mayhem when reason and prudence dictated otherwise. He went to places from which his own big-wave colleagues tried to warn him off. He slayed dragons. He loved all of it.

Chris Bertish charged, and he got some incredible rides, and he gave the photographers and video guys the opportunity to capture some amazing images. He also got mauled as a matter of course. He had suffered a torn medial collateral ligament in his left knee the year before. He had surfed one of the biggest Maverick's days that season with two cracked ribs; he simply covered his torso in tightly wound layers of cling wrap, zipped his wetsuit, and went out. He had been thrashed and rent, held underwater by the force of the wave so many times that he was well acquainted with the early stages of blackout—that calm, peaceful feeling that passed over him as he began to fade into unconsciousness. He knew how to fight that feeling long enough to survive being forced underwater by the power of a wave. He knew how to win.

He accepted getting beaten up by the ocean now and then. It was all part of the exchange for the type of surfing he most loved, an all-out style that included taking on the most difficult breaks on their least appealing days. Chris went after all of them, at Jaws and Waimea in Hawaii, at the menacing Dungeons in his native South Africa, at Todos Santos in Mexico, and, for the past several years, at Maverick's. Even when his friends begged him to back off once in a while—"Live to surf another day!" they told him—he had a hard time tugging on the reins. The thrill and the rush of going for it were impossible to capture in any other facet of his waking life. And to successfully chase that rush, he first needed the dream of a perfectly executed ride, one that was in harmony with the force of the wave itself.

Bertish was no kamikaze surfer. He wasn't trying to prove some point about himself by flinging his board down the sides of these liquid mountains. He was tremendously skilled and lived by the credos that he so often espoused to other people.

He told anyone who would listen how much he hated words like "can't" and "impossible." On his web site he embraced the notion of leaving one's comfort zone as often as possible. He had created his own company. He wasn't afraid of proselytizing his positive-energy theory of life, particularly the idea of creative visualization, of seeing a glorious result before one actually attained it. He believed in it and he practiced it. And because he was Chris Bertish and not someone else—with his trim, athletic build, gentle eyes, sloping nose, and salt-swept hair, with his Cape Town accent and a surfboard at his side—the words came off as heartfelt and soulful rather than greeting-card empty. You only had to see him in the water to know he meant everything he said.

But now, just now, lying in the pitch darkness of the living room of Jeff Clark's condominium that practically overlooked Pillar Point Harbor and the Maverick's wave beyond, it wasn't working. Even in his own vision, the wave kept winning. It was a bump that got him, every single time. Halfway down the face of the wave Chris could see that bump, a sudden churn in the water. It was like riding your bike over a pothole or a speed bump, depending on which way the water was moving. And every time he hit it, Chris was surfing so stiffly that he lost control of the board, couldn't complete the drop, and took the fall—and, God, the fall was crushing, like face-planting into cement and then being jackhammered to the bottom of the ocean. Chris had felt that before, many times, but the cold and unforgiving Half Moon Bay was different. Nobody wanted to know the darkness of the ocean floor when a Maverick's wave was slamming him down there.

But it was going to happen again and again in the vision because Chris was surfing stiff, and that wasn't the Bertish way. He could not go after the waves he wanted to get if he was surfing like that. He had to stay loose, stay flexible. He had to be made of rubber, be able to absorb those bumps under his board like the shocks absorbed the rough road under a car. Elasticity of body and mind was all. It was what could get him through, that elasticity. It had always gotten him through. He had to flow with the wave, because even the giant waves, even the 60-footers, had a flow to them that lay beyond their sheer power. It was a matter of becoming part of that flow, not fighting against it. Simply balling his fists and raging down the wave face would get him nowhere, and might get him killed. Even a major charger like Bertish was ultimately at the mercy of nature. He tried to focus.

Exhaustion was beginning to creep in; he needed badly to rest. Out at the edge of the harbor, the lighthouse at Pillar Point sounded its warning horn in a constant, doleful rhythm. But Chris could not sleep until he had this thing right. He had traversed half the planet to make it to the contest, and it might be his last such trip. The money for these adventures was quite completely gone. Chris was tired of begging family and friends for plane fare, as he had done so many times before, and they probably were tapped out anyway. The company back in Cape Town, CMB Agencies, which handled the marketing and branding of a number of surf-related outfits, was his own. He could miss only so many days of work, and he certainly couldn't afford to run up the travel charges against his own business. It all felt doubly true those times when

Chris came to California and then somehow got shorted on the experience—or, for that matter, never got to surf at all because the event was canceled. It had happened in the past and it could happen again. If he didn't nail it at Maverick's this year, then it was over. So be it.

The 2010 contest had denatured into a morass of politics that had forced the twenty-four elite competitors to argue and decide among themselves when to call the event, and under what circumstances. It was crazy, a massive waste of time. And it sat on top of the toll taken on Chris by the many false alarms over the years. A guy from South Africa couldn't just jump on a plane because the waves got tasty all of a sudden and the contest organizer decided to flash the green light. As much as he treasured it all, there was a limit to what he could really do, and there were other places to surf, with much better odds of a good day. All in all, it looked like this year would be his final sendoff in Northern California, after ten years pursuing a berth in the contest. He would spend his last few days celebrating with old friends in the water, the last few nights carousing with his buddies at the bars. As good as it felt, Chris could also sense the rest of his life beckoning.

At age thirty-five, he was as good a big-wave surfer as he had ever been in his life, but it didn't mean he would chase water-walls around the planet forever. Chris wasn't a kid. Every week, every day, was now precious. This Saturday in Half Moon Bay he would face his most elusive target, the Maverick's competition. While it might not constitute the end of the road, it suddenly felt like he could see it from here. And if that was the case, then this was the wave, this one inside his mind that he couldn't solve. He had to ride it tonight or he would never stand a chance of surviving it tomorrow—and this could be *the* wave, the one that decided whether he made it through the contest or not. Chris lay down and closed his eyes. It was time to run the sequence one more time, and then again, and again and again if he needed to. He had to get it right.

Get elastic, he thought to himself. Be a rubber man and get through it. He tried to imagine himself getting tossed around without losing control. He tried to make his mind refocus until it showed his legs taking the hit from the sucking, churning chunk of water. He needed to feel the board absorb the blows. He ran the sequence again. Again.

And, finally, it was there. He felt and saw a solid and continuous flow. Time slowed down as he cut across the yawning face of the wave. When he hit the suck-out area, he was flexible and easy through the turbulence; he was a rubber man. And then he was past it and intact. As the wave began to loom over him, forming a green-black wall of pressure that cast its massive shadow across everything, he saw himself slicing safely through to the breaking edge of the thickening barrel. The wave threw, heaving itself heavenward and then forward as the bottom began to drop out, the floor of the wave getting sucked back up into the curl, preparing to slam down its hundreds of thousands of gallons of force into the water that remained on the reef. But Chris already was on the giant. He was in it, cutting toward the far edge, skimming down the face, seeing the shoulder beyond. He blasted right through the curl, seconds ahead of the crush at each interval. He could feel the pull of nature, and he could hear nothing but the roar overhead, and he was a part of it.

Chris Bertish opened his eyes in the darkness; he was there on Jeff Clark's couch. He expelled a long breath and glanced out the window toward Clark's deck, to the ocean beyond. He was spending the night before the biggest day of his life in the home of the original Maverick's legend, and it was all going to happen for him. Chris wouldn't die. He wouldn't fail. He would absolutely, positively make it. He had seen it. It was all there, like a glorious beyond. Now he could sleep.

Chapter 2

A LITTLE BEFORE 5:30 A.M. ON THE morning of February 13, Greg Long emerged from his room at the Oceano Hotel, padded down the silent hallway and outside into the chilled air, and headed for a boat. Maverick's was blowing up—big, nasty, icy, magnificent—and Greg needed to go see. Among those joining him were his buddy Grant "Twiggy" Baker, Hawaiian mainstay Dave Wassel, and Greg's older brother, Rusty Long. Rusty, an accomplished rider and a favorite among his peers for his breakneck style and a willingness to charge that was just this side of crazy, had not been selected by Jeff Clark as one of The 24, the two dozen contestants awarded berths into Maverick's. Instead, he was on the list of alternates standing by if someone got hurt or failed to reach Half Moon Bay in time for the first heat. But being an alternate didn't mean Rusty was not going to surf Maverick's on this day. He just had to pick his spots.

Dawn, before the contestants got on the water, was one of those spots, and Rusty wasn't the only one with that idea. By the time he and a few others jumped out of the boat and began paddling for the wave, nearly a dozen riders were in the lineup. Greg, Twiggy, and Wassel weren't on their boards; they had come to learn what awaited them in their heats later that morning. What they saw was breathtaking: from the first minute of the first ride in that first light of morning, Mavs was going off. It threw itself over in 50-foot heaves, cartoonishly huge liquid arcs that looked like horseshoes of water turned on their sides. The sheer size and heaviness of the icy barrels virtually ensured that any conversation this morning would focus on the naked power of nature and, most likely, the clear frailty of man. Greg smiled to himself all the same. The opportunity was there for something insane to happen. And insane, for a rider who made a living hopping on a board, was a very good thing.

At twenty-six, Long already was firmly established as one of the megastars on the big-wave scene. Very significantly, he was one of the thimbleful of riders who actually got paid for their efforts. Born and raised in a surf-hungry family in San Clemente in Southern California, a son of the chief ranger at San Onofre State Beach, Long was an amateur national champion by age nineteen and poised for a fabulous run on the competitive surf circuit. He easily could have turned pro, slashing his way through smaller waves for bigger purses. He could have traded on his looks and dark brown eyes to make money posing for surf ads. It was all there to be had. But Greg was headed in another direction. He chose to ride the liquid mountains.

When he first showed up at Maverick's in 2004, that choice led to a quick and complete acceptance by the break's longtime surfers. Though at the time he was only twenty, Greg was embraced by the Mavs riders who quickly saw in him the better parts of themselves. Long had the ability and the connections to big-time it, and yet he wanted to go around the world chasing the largest, gnarliest sets he could find. While his abundant talent was visible to anyone with surf knowledge almost, he approached the days and the waves with a humility and generous spirit that endeared him to even the most scarred veterans. He hadn't an ounce of brag in him; he simply surfed lights-out.

Greg showed up at Maverick's both because it scared him and because he loved it, just as he routinely trekked to Dungeons in South Africa for weeks at a time, pitting himself against the wave and slowly, inexorably creating new boundaries of what was considered possible. He exuded the quiet calm of a person who knew exactly what he wanted to do, yet he attacked the waves with the enthusiasm of a kid on his first ride. Afterward, it was all smiles and gratefulness. It was the perfect combination.

Long had made his first big-wave foray at age fifteen, pulling into a series of huge breaks at Todos Santos in Mexico. He was eighteen when the Red Bull Big Wave Africa contest beckoned; he won the event his second year surfing it. He won a Billabong XXL Global Big Wave Award for somehow pulling through a 65-foot ride at Dungeons, and there certainly was no question about his bona fides. But until Greg broke through at Maverick's, he felt that he had a hole in his résumé—and on a contest day at Pillar Point, such a breakthrough often proved elusive. Twice he went out in the first round. Once, in 2005, he came close, scoring a perfect ten on a ride in his first heat, but he finished second overall behind Anthony Tashnick, the only surfer in the lineup who was younger than Long. It wasn't until 2008 that the opportunity to really succeed at Maverick's finally presented itself, and it was a day when Long's character was put on full display, along with that of some of the biggest names in the sport.

That January, Long made it to the finals along with Grant Washburn, Twiggy Baker, Jamie Sterling, Evan Slater, and Tyler Smith—a collection of intense, decorated riders. Sitting out on the water together during the last heat, a heavy silence lay upon the lineup. It was a rare case: the group felt the peculiar tension of actual competition. That included Long, who had to that point played a conservative hand that day, slipping into the semifinals in third place in his heat and then making the finals while being obscured by the all-out performance of Hawaiian Jamie Sterling. Despite it, Greg felt strong, in control. He had the sense that he was one good wave away from winning it all, and he was willing to wait through the entire finals session to get that wave. But the idea of taking top money in such a star-studded field struck him as faintly misguided.

Almost all of the surfers' time was normally spent in undiluted support of one another, often of a literal fashion, with some surfers offering to ride the Jet Ski safety patrol so that others could catch a few waves. It felt strange and a bit uneasy to be openly trying to outduel each other for the $30,000 top prize. And for Greg, who had chosen this life over more promising money on the pro tour, the idea of suddenly competing for a check put a spin on the afternoon that made it a bit less joyful—not beyond redemption, by any means, but a little less fun than it could be. It sounded silly to be perplexed about getting paid, but such was the vibe.

The cash brought with it a level of professionalism and win-the-money competitiveness in which many of the surfers had minimal interest. They didn't *want* to be pros in the classic sense. All of them wanted great rides, certainly, and there were both friendly and edgy rivalries on display that had been years in the making. Undoubtedly, for some of the people who jetted in for the contest, producing a great individual effort with all the cameras rolling could have a potential bankroll effect. But in general, the group was not comprised of money surfers. For most of them, most of the time, getting on the water meant hustling in some precious time between job shifts, or on a "sick day," or on the weekend or vacation. Some of them, the hardcore Northern California element of the sport, had crafted most of the rest of their lives around the notion that it was the surf, and the lifestyle it offered, that they valued above everything else. It was low-money by definition, and that was part of what made the surf spot so pure and so real—you had to *want* it.

Most of the surfers were willing to slap a company's decal on their boards in exchange for a buck or two, but many of them felt that the contest lately was becoming a vehicle for the marketing of a brand. The surfers clearly had struggled for years to reconcile the reality of the business grind with the sense of freedom they had always experienced on the water. Now, they were being watched, judged, and paid. There had always been a feeling among some of the older guard at Mavs—rock-solid godfathers like Doc Renneker—that the injection of money into the surf equation was disastrous by any measure. Now, sitting out in the lineup, Greg Long and his colleagues found themselves in what was, for them as surfers, a most unusual position.

As they waited for the sets to roll in, Long tried to break the mood. He thought about what he wanted to say, and he made a light comment about simply pooling the top-six prize money ($57,000 in total) and splitting it, regardless of the final placements. It was thrown out as conversation amid the eerie quiet of an unusually uneventful contest, the surfers at that moment sitting on calm water with no decent waves in sight. It also was not groundbreaking, but rather in the tradition of a similar group decision reached years earlier by Greg, Twiggy Baker, Chris Bertish, and others at an event in South Africa. But Greg's words resonated with Twiggy, who had proposed the same thing here only a couple of years earlier to no avail. A conversation ensued, unbeknownst to the rest of the world. Hands were joined, a circle formed. And when the men came in from Maverick's later that afternoon, they announced their decision to those on the beach.

By the time they did, Greg had put on a show. Waiting patiently in the final heat, he saw every other surfer grab a wave before he did; but when his water-wall arrived it was a beast, a 40-footer on a too-calm day that arced so radically Long felt himself losing contact with his board on his way down the face. He held on, rode the wave all the way out, and emerged with a perfect ten score from the judges. When Long later added an extended ride in which he outran the whitewater as it tried to chase him down, he sewed up the title that perhaps meant the most to him. He had surfed Mavs well in front of his best friends.

The trophy scene was a classic moment, as Long and the others explained what they had decided to the thunderous applause of those gathered on the beach to celebrate. All six riders took home enough money—$9,500—to make it an amazing day. It was, ultimately, their way of receiving the first-place reward without endorsing the idea behind it. At the suggestion of Long, the youngest of the bunch but also one of the few big-wavers who could really be considered a professional, the group remained in an all-for-one formation. The kid had the right idea.

Greg had long since been declared an honorary old man. In every way that mattered, he was an ancient soul. Despite his being younger than Rusty, it was Greg who played the role of decision-making adult in their surfing relationship. Greg made the calls, for the most part, on where and when to hunt the biggest prizes among the massive waves around the world. He followed the weather and wave patterns with religious fervor but scientific curiosity, and he had become one of the leading voices of the Maverick's movement toward global recognition despite not being a local. Other surfers found themselves trusting Greg's judgment and asking him questions, even though many of them had ridden at Mavs for years before he came on the scene. When it came time to make a final call on whether to hold the contest, Jeff Clark had Greg on his very short list of people to consult. Long spent hours and days studying the point, the breaks, and the conditions. When he left Half Moon Bay, it was usually in order to get himself to the waves that were breaking in Hawaii or South Africa or Peru or Mexico, or else he was headed to a new frontier, like Ireland, where word had come around of a reef capable of producing 100-foot sets. An inveterate sojourner on the big-wave trail, the amount of respect Greg was accorded by the group was so great it was difficult to gauge.

His relationship with Twiggy was the leavening in the bread. Unlike Long, Grant "Twiggy" Baker had come to the big-wave hunt late in his surfing life. Beginning in 2008, at age thirty-five, he was for the first time seriously sponsored to surf. He had nearly a decade on Greg, but in almost every other respect it was Twig who seemed the younger. Greg Long, for all his love of the pure release of surfing, was nevertheless studious and calculating in his choices. Baker, a South African rider of irrepressible spirit, was more inclined to say yes immediately—to whatever—and sort out later whether it'd been a mistake. Both were clearly surfers in look and style, though Twig was the scruffy one, walking around with a shock of unruly hair and a two-day growth of stubble on his chin. Having only found big-wave nirvana past age thirty, he was committed to making the proceedings a good time on top of the serious business of riding giant water-walls all over the world. With Twig, the fun showed up everywhere that he did.

"It's true that Twiggy's past thirty-five now, which is pretty old to be a young guy on the circuit," a fellow surfer said with a chuckle. "But it's okay, because he's really immature."

In temperament and pace, Long and Baker often seemed diametrically opposed; but in fact they were global travelers together, almost inseparable. Their commonalities far outweighed the differences in their personalities. Greg and Twiggy were two of the only sponsored big-wave surfers who actually earned enough from endorsement deals to make surfing their full-time gigs. They spent days, weeks, and months getting themselves to the places where the waves were biggest and the photographers and videographers most present. Being seen was part of the deal. As much as each of them loved to ride a wave for the pure pleasure of it, and as often as they were willing to do so without any fanfare, the truth was that the cameras practically went everywhere they did. That much was just plain business.

While Long built his reputation over years and years of brilliant work, Twiggy had burst onto the scene thanks to a huge boost from Maverick's. Baker's first visit to Half Moon Bay came in 2004, after years of killing big waves at places like Dungeons in his homeland. It was Long and a few others from Southern California, people who had often surfed Dungeons and gotten to know Twiggy there, who finally prevailed on him to make the trip.

"They said, 'Come on over for a couple of weeks,'" Twiggy said. "They said they had big waves. I never believed it."

It didn't take long for Baker to change his mind. During the first session that Baker ever attempted at Mavs, Twiggy experienced the peculiar sensation of watching the bottom literally drop out of the massive wave he was attempting to ride. It is a trait of the site. As the wave lunges up out of the deep water, it appears at first to have established itself completely, but the reef below is not quite finished concentrating and funneling the swell's power into a single, brutal throw. At the point where a normal wave reaches its apex and a surfer sets his feet and starts to turn and ride, a Maverick's wave often unexpectedly continues to rise—or drop, depending on which end of the telescope you feel like peering through. Looking down from the lip of the wave, it appears that all of the water is being sucked out of the ocean in front and powered into the barrel behind. As it becomes demonstrably taller and, however briefly, less concave, the wave appears to rise up out of the ocean floor, which has the simultaneous effect of dropping the bottom out of it. If you're the surfer on the board already committed to skimming down the face, the sensation is that of being inside an elevator when the cable suddenly snaps. It's a free fall straight down the front. Many of the most notorious wipeout photos at Maverick's—like the one that made sixteen-year-old Jay Moriarity an international poster boy for the dangers of the wave in 1994—have captured this phenomenon: a rider coming down a wave so steep that he has physically lost contact with his board. It isn't a pretty landing.

Twiggy Baker encountered precisely this kind of wave on his very first ride, with the master Jeff Clark sitting only a few yards away on the shoulder of the break, observing the newcomer. Twig's reaction to the predicament would set the tone for almost everything he subsequently achieved at the site. "He almost got totally smashed," Washburn said, remembering the story one evening while Baker sat in a nearby chair, working on a Bloody Mary and grinning widely. "When that thing starts lifting and then keeps on lifting right as you're trying to turn, you'll get stuck up at the top and just thrown off the side. At that point, if you do anything other than go straight down, you're going to get smashed. And he was right there. I'm thinking, 'Oh, no, he's going to eat it right in front of Jeff.' And then he didn't. Instead of doing anything else, he just went in a free fall straight down. It was exactly the right thing to do. It was clear that the guy had it, because you either do it that way or you don't do it right."

Washburn laughed. "Jeff was like, 'Who's that guy?' And I said, 'I thought I told you. He's from South Africa. He's really good.'"

Twiggy really was good, and he really was on his way. Later that season, in the winter of 2004–05, he was the very last addition to Clark's deep list of alternates to the contest, which earned him a free flight to California. The next season he was awarded a spot in the lineup, thanks to the fans' write-in vote on the Maverick's web site, and in the winter of 2006, at the Maverick's Surf Contest, Grant "Twiggy" Baker broke it open internationally. He staggered a field chock full of superstars in the sport: Santa Cruz charger Tyler Smith; Hawaii legend Brock Little; Matt Ambrose of Pacifica, considered by many to be one of Mavs' godfathers; *Surfer* magazine editor and famed rider Evan Slater; and Washburn. When Twiggy rode a wave in his first heat to a perfect ten score, it was clear that what Jeff Clark and Washburn had seen on Baker's first day was no optical illusion. He was fearless and accomplished. It was a day that put Baker on the map and launched him toward his eventual sponsorship. And were it not for that very first ride on his very first day at Pillar Point, Baker might not ever have made a contest appearance at Maverick's.

"One wave changed my life," Twiggy said. "If I had fallen on that wave, right in front of Jeff, I would never have been invited to the contest. I might never have come back."

Washburn leaned forward in his chair. "If you'd fallen, you might never *want* to come back."

"It was that close," Twiggy said. "I was close to not making it. I remember it clear as day. I'd been watching for about half an hour, working my way up there. For some reason, a modest wave came through at once, and suddenly I was the only person out there in position, and the wave came through. I had to get it. I *had* to get it." So he did.

Now, in the early light of February 13, 2010, Twiggy and Greg were simply two more of the Mavs mainstays, doing their diligence on the wave, getting prepped for the day to come. It was left to Rusty and Kohl Kristensen and Mark Healy and some of the other riders, the alternates and the guys who simply loved to surf the point and wanted some of the action, to make that first foray. Early on, Rusty jumped up on a giant breaker and, with his brother and others shouting him on, tried to set his inside rail. The wave would have none of it. It suddenly grew several feet, launched itself forward, and buried the surfer in a pounding series of hold-downs. Washed and spun well toward the rocks near the beach, Rusty came up safely, but the message was clear. It was going to be an enormous, dangerous day.

How big, exactly, was a notion best left to the surfers themselves. If you're the person on shore, straining to get a decent look at the riders half a mile out to sea, you might easily mistake a 40-foot wave for a 30-footer; but for the people actually trying to traverse the face of one of the giants at Maverick's, differences of mere feet can have tremendous implication, especially if that extra lift is a late-blooming development that alters the arc of the wave.

The language of the big-wave surfers takes into account the true size of a swell in quaint fashion: by attempting to minimize it. Although the heights in this book are put at actual value, few riders ever speak of waves in such terms. Instead, they adopt the so-called Hawaiian scale of wave modesty, cutting the estimate by half, so the story goes, in order to lessen the intimidation factor. Thus, a 40-foot wave is called a 20-footer. If they're surfing "fifteens," it means that the wave's ultimate height is closer to 30 feet by the time the face fully reveals itself. Halving the estimate puts the wave back into a reasonable, survivable dimension.

On contest day 2010, there was no mistaking it. Maverick's was kicking big, and longtime surfers of the point could also tell that the wave was transferring an inordinate amount of energy. The sets were packing an extra punch; they were even thicker and more brutally forceful than usual. In the parlance of the surfers, they were heavy. It wasn't just the added height, though that alone was both terrifying and alluring. It had to do with the sheer tonnage of water and the force of the throw involved when the wave came blasting up off the ski-ramp reef below. It was an expression of uniquely concentrated energy, and for many that energy had a sinister aspect. It was a voodoo wave. The surfers approached, as they would all day, with a mixture of nervous excitement and utter respect. It was the kind of day where even a moderate miscalculation could get them seriously mangled.

Twiggy had always thought that the contest day was, in many respects, the safest day of the year at Mavs. The surfers were virtually surrounded by onlookers, photographers, Jet Ski rescue craft, and the like. If somebody got in trouble or found himself pinned down in a two- or three-wave hold, he would most likely surface to find help all around him. Of course, that only addressed after-the-fact emergencies. The other side of any day's coin was risk, and the primary factor in the amount of risk taken on contest day was, well, the contest. Even men like these, who clearly valued other things above money, could find themselves taking chances they wouldn't normally take, especially with a $50,000 payout for the top prize. For many of the surfers, $50,000 was more than they would make in a year or even in a couple of years—and certainly more than they would ever make for surfing, period. It was life-changing money in that it could buy them time, and time to surf was the one thing none of them had enough of.

Given the amount of money in play, there was no doubt that several of the guys would be willing to test waves that on any other day they'd respectfully pass. It was no small risk. The one true lifetime mistake you could make at Maverick's, aside from having no business being out there in the first place, was to get it in your mind that you were going to "take on" the wave. There was no taking on Maverick's. A surfer either became part of the wave, and thus survived it and learned to coexist with and appreciate it, or he battled against it and lost horribly. The history of the place suggested no third outcome.

Watching his brother navigate the giant early-morning waves, Greg Long looked on carefully, making mental notes. Nearby, Twiggy spoke in a low voice, nearly reverential. They were awed by what they were seeing. The two of them had surfed Maverick's so many times that, even though they'd caught huge rides here before, each of them knew he was witnessing the start of a special day. It was size and it was dynamics, and it was the period, too—sets of three and four waves each were pounding in from the open ocean one after another, with almost no time separating them. To see the two of them conferring, exchanging first-glance knowledge and discussing wave height and break and other elemental factors, was to realize how laughably out of touch with reality the established stereotype of the surfer had become. As much as they loved surfing, Twig and Greg were students of the game. They were into wave patterns, weather technology, buoy readings. This was fun, but serious fun. It was the new edge of surfing: a host of great riders, but shockingly few dudes.

The stereotyped image of the surfer almost never applied to the big-wave masters at Maverick's, anyway. For one thing, the lineup at Mavs tended to skew way older than at other, more routinely surfed breaks. Like some of the other big-wave sites around the world, Half Moon Bay was the kind of place that rewarded intelligence, patience, calculation, and cunning, all of which generally were the province of veteran experience. Maverick's had a habit of pounding the life out of the young guns who showed up thinking they'd rock the place or surf it hard. The short history of the site was absolutely filled with stories of guys who came out for one winter, went after Maverick's like crazy, and then never showed up again. They were spent, beat up, blown out. Surfing the break was all about picking your spots, knowing when to lay off, knowing when to go.

While there were still some brilliant young surfers dotting the lineup, it was no coincidence that many of the most highly regarded riders were those of a deep-veteran status, guys in their late thirties, mid-forties, and beyond, people like Grant Washburn and Peter Mel—and Clark himself, still pushing at fifty-two, using all of that wave savvy to maximize his stoke and minimize his exposure to Mavs' dark side. For all who rode the wave, having big balls and an addiction to risk-taking were a given, not some sort of revelation. Beyond that, it came down to life lessons and smarts. Maverick's was a natural force born of a natural formation, but it also was a major psychological and physical barrier. Scores of people who marched into other tough waves up and down the North Coast wouldn't even consider attempting the outside bowls at Mavs. It was like a forbidden land. And those who cherished the wave were perfectly all right with that.

"One of the big questions is, what keeps everybody else from doing it? Because one of the things we like about it is that nobody else is doing it," one surfer said. "If there were a hundred people out there instead of five or ten, then we don't want to be out there. All of the paddle-in big-wave guys are really into pushing out the frontiers of what is possible—but most of what they like about it is there's nobody else out there, you know? It's fun to be with your friends, and it's fun to be in your small group."

The risk was real, and not just on a day like today, when Greg and Twiggy could see immediately that the chances they were going to take would be abnormally fraught. Every Maverick's surfer who lasted more than one season at the point understood the dynamic. Grant Washburn had surfed it more often than anyone over the past several years, and he had reached a place in his life where he simply wasn't interested in taking the most extreme chances it offered. Attempting the wave on any true Maverick's day was enough; the rewards were psychic and spiritual and renewable. Contest day produced in him a deeply mixed emotion.

"A lot of days you can surf it safely, but on the contest day, with all that money out there and all those people watching and taking footage, you are setting safety aside. And they're not going to get you if you get knocked unconscious and don't come back up to the surface," Washburn said. "They can't get you until you come to the top, and if you don't come up . . ."

He let his voice trail off. "It's pretty hard to find people, even when they're up and waving. If you are underwater and somebody's not looking specifically for you, it's bad—and even if they are, they might not find you until it's too late. There are about ten ways to get buried out here, and the impact zone is so intense. I mean, Greg broke his ankle on a six-foot wave—just a six-footer. It doesn't take much. A guy separated his shoulder on a four-foot wave. You're not talking about height; you're talking about energy. If you get a 20-footer that breaks down on you, you're going to get hurt."

There was no such thing as an easy wave at Maverick's. Mark Foo's death in 1994 should have taught everyone that, if it taught them nothing else. Even the seemingly routine wave was freighted with danger and full of power. It was not a surf break for ordinary people, which was one of the reasons people like Greg Long and Twiggy Baker and Grant Washburn and Chris Bertish found themselves drawn to it.

Now, on the morning of the great day, as the sun continued to make its slow pass above the hills just east of Pillar Point, Greg, Twiggy, Rusty, and the rest made their way back to the harbor. They had the feeling that something unforgettable was about to happen. A few hours later, in those first few panicked moments after Chris Bertish went down under a wave and didn't come back up, they would begin to understand just how right they were.

Chapter 3

HE PLACE THEY CALL MAVERICK'S IS a surf point in the same way that the 1927 New York Yankees were a baseball team. From San Francisco, the point is accessible via a 22-mile regimen of twists and turns along Highway 1, through Pacifica, and down a particularly malicious piece of road around an area known as the Devil's Slide, past which the pavement suddenly smooths and broadens out to the finish, a breathtaking stretch in which the ocean thrusts itself into full view, the waves crashing home along the broken shores of the rugged, rock-strewn beaches of Northern California.

In the geography of surfing, Maverick's is nowhere. The spot lies well south of San Francisco's Ocean Beach, home to some of the truly fine surfers of the area, and an hour's drive north of Santa Cruz, where so many of the hard chargers cut their teeth at Steamer Lane, Cowell's, and other storied surf points. Barely visible from the highway, and even then only if you know exactly when and where to look, Maverick's is a classic don't-blink proposition for most travelers.

In terms of access, the place is more remote yet. To even get to the bluff from which the wave-break can be studied, a visitor first has to cut through tiny Princeton by the Sea, known simply as Princeton to the locals, whose scattered homes and condos comprise an unincorporated hamlet at the farthest northern reaches of Half Moon Bay. There are a couple of hotels and bed-and-breakfasts, several bars and restaurants, a lighthouse, and the tranquil harbor itself. A few blocks away, on a thin reed of side street called Harvard Avenue, sits the building that for years housed the original Maverick's Surf Shop, Jeff Clark's longtime storefront. A rusted-out SUV is usually parked in front, telltale surfboards mounted on top. Several hundred yards beyond, you abandon your car at the dirt and gravel lot off Pillar Point, and leg out the last half mile to the bluff itself.

Back in the early days, when Clark was first bringing the wave to the rest of the surfing world, you could scramble up the side of that bluff and, after walking for a few yards on flat ground, grab hold of the post of an old chicken-wire fence that jutted out almost off the edge of the property. With a good jump you could swing, fireman's-pole style, to the other side. If you lost your footing, or your grip, it was about a 60-foot drop onto the slicing beach boulders below, but the reward for the risk was spectacular. A fat expanse of land led to the far edge of the bluff and a sensational, sidelong view of Maverick's. A few years ago the U.S. Air Force, which owns the land, declared it off-limits to the general public; and by 2010 it was allowed to be used only on contest day, and then only by the judges and a few select members of the media. Speaking practically, maybe thirty people could crowd onto that very first patch of bluff before the fenced-off area, and the quality of the view from there was entirely dependent on the weather conditions and where the riders had chosen to sit on the wave.

In short, there is no really good way to view Maverick's except on the water or perhaps overhead. Contrast this to Hawaii's famed Waimea Bay, where the huge rollers are easily seen and fully appreciated, and it is no surprise that Maverick's, as both a phenomenon and a planned destination, eluded the grasp of the world's greatest big-wave surfers for decades. Forget being on their collective radar; the spot wasn't really even on a map. Even after Jeff Clark "discovered" the break in the 1970s, it would be another fifteen years before any of the renowned giant-riders so much as gave the wave a passing sniff, let alone suited up and attempted to navigate it. Maverick's was a secret lying in open water, and Clark was the only person who seemed able, or willing, to find it.

Clark grew up in Half Moon Bay, a few miles south of Pillar Point, and he spent many of his formative years living in his family's home at Miramar Beach, with the waves right in front of him and a surfboard almost always at the ready. It was routine for him to hop on a board and catch a few rides before or after school, preferably both; and as time passed, Clark's taste for the waves grew to a full hunger. He needed a bigger, more quality stoke than what he was getting outside his front door, and he chased up and down the Northern

California coastline exploring what the ocean had to offer. He was both fearless and respectful, and he seemed able to find a good surf day in the most mediocre of conditions. It was, to him, all part of the experience of reaching higher and striving for more. From his first days at Half Moon Bay High School in the 1970s onward, Jeff sought the bigger wave, and then the one that was bigger after that. It wasn't long before his attention was drawn to the monster that appeared to break way out in the middle of the water.

The scientific and historical explanations of Maverick's are detailed, brilliant, and ever-evolving; the short version is that it is flat out one of the most insane surf points in the world. What Clark and his high-school buddies saw, as they first peered at the coast from the bluff above, was a wave of such seemingly supernatural force that it was easily visible to them despite being closed off to the view of those driving on the nearby highway. The extent of his friends' interest in the giant wave ran to the bluff, but no closer. Only Clark spent even a few minutes trying to discern how the wave actually broke and how it might be ridden. No one else was considering it. The classmates came and went, usually in his company. Clark stayed, cinching up his hooded sweatshirt against the elements and squatting on the bluff day after day, peering through the cloud cover and the fog and chill to the rough surf, watching the wave throw itself over in corded, muscular sets. The more time he spent looking at the wave, the more intrigued he became with the idea that there was a way to find harmony within it, on a board.

As it happened, he wasn't the first to wonder.

Long before Maverick's had a name, it certainly was a place. All of the inherent conditions that today create the waves that people like Clark and Peter Mel and Greg Long live to ride existed thousands of years before. But there is no history to suggest that anyone was daring enough to try the waves on a surfboard until 1961, a mere fourteen years before Jeff Clark would take his fateful first run as a teenager.

In March of '61, three surfers took their boards, walked to the far edge of Pillar Point, and gazed out at the break. The surfers' names were Jim Thompson, Dick Knottmeyer, and Alex Matienzo, and they brought company: a white-haired German shepherd who belonged to Matienzo's roommate in San Francisco. The dog answered to the name Maverick. The men put their boards in the water and started to paddle out. Maverick, who often swam and played in the surf with her owner or with Matienzo, happily jumped in to tag along. Matienzo quickly concluded that it was no safe place for the shepherd, and he took Maverick back to shore and leashed her to the bumper of a car. Returning to the surf, Matienzo joined the other two men in trying to solve the puzzle of the spot's complicated wave breaks.

The men surfed the smaller inner reef for a while, catching a few of the lesser peaks about a quarter mile offshore, where the waves broke just overhead. The conditions were brutal, and together they made a collective decision that the stuff farther out—another quarter mile, at least, where the true reef-ramp resides—was too dangerous to be messed with. Reluctantly, they headed back in after a session that could mostly be described as interesting, brief, and mediocre.

Back on dry land, the three decided to christen the break by naming it after the dog, since Maverick appeared to have had the best time out there among all of them. Maverick's Point was born, later shortened to Maverick's and, since then, stripped of the apostrophe as often as not for simplicity's sake. Still, Maverick's it truly is. Finished for the day, the group headed back to the city, likely quite unaware that they had made a small bit of history. Thompson, Knottmeyer, and Matienzo had stumbled on a topographical and meteorological fluke, and unwittingly exposed the complex, evolving science of the Maverick's wave.

Still, for nearly a decade and a half after that, curiosity about the surf point appeared to diminish into nothingness. That's not to say that no one ever stuck a board in the water out there—in the special features section of the film *Riding Giants*, for example, Jeff Clark recalls his Little League coach taking the players out to the surf point, which he, too, called Maverick's, to ride the smaller inside waves—but there is nothing in the oral or written history of the place to suggest that anyone left a mark. From what little is known of the intervening years that Jeff spent on the bluff, gazing out at the vicious sea that sprawled below him, Maverick's appears to have been ceded back to nature.

Clark never intended to change that. He found himself looking for a way to connect with, and perhaps become a small part of, the unpredictable surf, not to claim dominion over it. He wanted to feel the power of the wave, to be reminded of his minuscule place in the universe. It sounded mostly spiritual and only a little bit surfer-ish, and several of his friends thought he was crazy. In retrospect, he most certainly was.

Watch any of the major surfing sessions at Mavs today, and they're attended by a virtual phalanx of safety, rescue, tow-in, and recording apparatuses: guys on personal watercraft, photo and video crews, the Harbor Patrol. Nobody goes alone, or at least very few of the experienced surfers do. Maverick's is one of those places in which time spent on the wave actually engenders more caution, not less; the elite surfers prefer to travel in packs, the better to look out for one another and be on hand if something truly hairy occurs. But Clark, at age seventeen, was so drawn to the wave that when the day finally occurred in 1975 that he sucked up his courage and paddled out, he went alone. A friend stayed on shore, refusing to accompany him but volunteering to call the Coast Guard in case somebody needed to come fish Clark's limp body out of the surf. It was the first time Clark surfed Maverick's by himself, and it represented the cutting edge of a fifteen-year trend.

Maverick's scares the hell out of people, and the ones whom it doesn't immediately scare come to respect it soon enough. Ben Marcus, a writer for *Surfer* magazine, visited the place in 1992 and described it as "gloomy, isolated, inherently evil," and on most days his foreboding is an understatement. The water temperature, already about 30 degrees colder than Hawaii's comparatively welcoming swells, feels more severe than other surf in Northern California, perhaps because of the 60-foot undersea drop-off just beyond the reef—a deep, frosty bowl into which unlucky riders get plunged by the pile driver they've just failed to negotiate. The surfers wear heavy neoprene wetsuits to enhance their chances in a horrible wipeout and to retain as much of their body heat as possible, but the thickness restricts movement, and the buoyancy of the suits makes it tougher to dive under waves.

Worse, though, are the hold-downs, when a fresh wave crashes on a surfer's head just as he is attempting to surface from his initial wipeout. Maverick's is infamous for the length, depth, and ferocity of its hold-downs, with the cold water testing the surfer's ability to hold his breath and the violence of the spin cycle leaving him disoriented and, occasionally, with punctured eardrums. At Mavs as elsewhere, the length of the trouble depends mostly on the period, or the number of seconds in between waves. A two-wave hold-down is common; a three-wave hold, though terrifying, is by no means unique.

The first time that Randy Cone rode a wave at Maverick's taught him all about it. "It was an evening in November '98," the veteran rider says immediately, remembering distinctly, as most surfers do, his initial trip to Pillar Point. Cone, a handyman from San Francisco, was using a new board that he had made just for the occasion. His craftsmanship appeared to pay off in his first session. Cone got up on the first wave he tried, scooting down the side of it in relative comfort, then making it safely out the side as the monster broke overhead. He felt the first rush of Maverick's special brand of intensity; it was intoxicating.

"And then," Cone says, "I got cocky."

His friends in the lineup told him not to attempt the next wave—it was too big and breaking too deep—but Cone didn't listen. He was full of himself and full of stoke, energized by the adrenaline surge of surfing a wave the size of some of the buildings he worked on. Cone went paddling after the swell his friends tried to talk him out of, but he started too far back, close to the peak. Before Cone knew what was happening he got caught inside the wave, which promptly sucked him up into its building barrel, then threw him "over the falls" and buried him deep in the impact zone. Thrashed around in the black wash, Cone struggled to get his bearings under a brutal hold-down. He fought the cold darkness, scrambled his way back to the surface. His breath came in jagged gasps.

"When I finally got up there, I saw my board," Cone said. "It was in pieces everywhere—it looked like a truck hit it. Somebody said, 'Welcome to Maverick's.'"

The piece of ocean that surrounds the break is a habitat for elephant seals and a migratory pass-through for great white sharks, which have been pulled out of the water around the wave with some regularity over the years. While no one has ever been attacked while in the Maverick's lineup itself, a few years ago a local named Tim West was paddling out when he suddenly was thrown skyward, away from his longboard, by an extraordinarily violent thump. When he got his head above water, West saw "this gray thing just thrashing my board." The subsequent tooth fragment found embedded in his ten-foot one-inch board was estimated by an expert to have come from a 12- to 14-foot white shark weighing about a ton.

And all of that is to say nothing of the Boneyard, the most shudder-inducing feature of the area. The Boneyard is the jagged inner reef of cut rocks and massive boulders, an absolutely unforgiving place on the Pillar Point map near the shoreline, and you get there only by extreme bad luck, flushed against it by the unrelenting afterwash of a wipeout. A surfer who falls early on a Mavs wave and gets sucked over the top, as Randy Cone did after he failed to navigate the tricky drop down the side, can find himself hurtled underwater in a sideways spin toward the rocks. Once there, successive waves essentially pin him in place, thrashing him again and again—getting rag-dolled, the surfers call it—until he can crawl up on one of the rocks and get out of the pounding wash, or perhaps receive a sled rescue from someone on a Jet Ski brave enough to venture into the zone. Broken bones, ripped suits, crushed boards—all are common currency at the Boneyard. "It's a worst-case scenario," says Bruce Jenkins, the renowned San Francisco sports columnist, who has written passionately and knowledgeably about Maverick's for twenty years. "A leash snaps, and you're just sitting there getting pounded by one wave after another as you go toward that pile of rocks. For most of us, that's simply, 'Well, no.'"

Jeff Clark said yes—not to the Boneyard specifically, but to the scene as a whole. He was so taken by the wave, and by the idea of being part of it, that he was willing to accept the risks even as he became vitally more aware of their scope and implications. As Jenkins puts it, "Jeff surfed it, but he surfed it out of pure love. It's not like he wanted to surf it all by himself for fifteen years. He asked people all the time, but nobody would go. And even Jeff didn't surf it all the time; it was closer to a few times a winter, because it's a fickle place and he was out there alone. He wasn't going out by himself on a stormy, kick-ass, you're-gonna-die day like twenty guys will do now—twenty guys all together. Jeff was picking his spots and being smart, and he still literally could not get anybody to go. And I don't blame them for not going."

An air of threat hangs over Maverick's, especially on the fog-shrouded, overcast Half Moon Bay days that pockmark the winter months. It is inescapable, but not enough to deter the most enthusiastic big-wave riders. (Of course, there are only 150 or so of those on the planet.) Mark Foo's shocking death in 1994 cemented the surf point as the kind of place that only the truly committed will dare, while at the same time exponentially increasing its international profile. It was in the wake of Foo's tragedy that Maverick's began to be understood as an equal alongside Waimea, Jaws, Dungeons, and the other classic big-wave locations around the world. It was huge and beautiful when it rolled and barreled, and the high of a good ride was enough to keep a surfer going for weeks and months afterward. But despite the brilliance and almost mystical, savage beauty of the wave, Maverick's has derived its greatest fame from what happens when things go bad.

Sitting in the living room of his house in Montara, a picturesque dot on the map between Pacifica and Half Moon Bay, Bruce Jenkins thumbs through the pages of the book that he edited with Grant Washburn. Entitled *Inside Maverick's*, the book features surf photographer Doug Acton's riveting visual tribute to the glory and the dark danger of the place, along with firsthand accounts by some of the wave's elite surfers and chroniclers. "It's the best wave in—well, some say the best in the world. But it's certainly the best wave in California,"

Jenkins says. "And Jeff did it all by himself for fifteen years. In the water, he's Sir Edmund Hillary. He's a true cut above. I've seen him surfing places all up and down the coast on gnarly, weird, horrible days, and he's out there just loving it."

From 1975 to 1990, Jeff Clark was the whole story. No one he spoke to about the place was willing to even acknowledge that it existed, much less suit up and get on a board with him. The locals in Ocean Beach and Santa Cruz scoffed at the idea that they had overlooked something as obvious as a place with North Shore–sized breakers, and the Hawaiians themselves found the whole thing inconceivable—and even if real, far too cold and menacing to bother with. Looking back, it's almost as if Clark created the point out of whole cloth.

On January 22, 1990, everything changed. That day, a huge northwest winter swell arrived in California, bringing with it redline surf conditions that sent jolts of anticipation through the locals. Clark, who was working a construction project in San Francisco, got the news, ran to his car, and headed for the water. The closest big location was Ocean Beach, but the scene there was already out of control: huge surf, even heavier choppy waves, and no way to paddle out. The storm was making entire sections of the coast unrideable. But Clark knew Maverick's, and he knew from his experience that the same swells that were destroying O.B. might produce perfect, clean barrels at Pillar Point. In the parking lot, he prevailed on two skeptical Santa Cruz surfers, Tom Powers and Dave Schmidt, to follow him down the highway. Lacking any decent alternative, they agreed. After a forty-five-minute drive, Clark walked them around the lagoon and up onto the bluff above Mavs so that they could get a look at the break. His "secret" would be kept no longer.

Dave Schmidt could not believe what was in front of him. He looked out several times to confirm the sight: the tubes at Maverick's were every bit the equal of Waimea, and of Hawaii's other massive surf points as well. It was a staggering revelation. Schmidt and Powers proceeded cautiously to follow Clark into the surf. Over the next few hours, every man caught at least a couple of waves, enough for the force and fury of the place to be brought home to Schmidt without any room for doubt. Schmidt's next call, appropriately enough, was to his brother. At the time, Richard Schmidt was easily the most accomplished big-wave rider in Northern California, a person who routinely spent three to six months a year surfing Hawaii's largest swells. In fact, he was in Hawaii, at the In Memory of Eddie Aikau Invitational, on the same day that all hell broke loose at Maverick's.

"I was there at the Eddie too that year," Bruce Jenkins says. "Richard is just a god over there, killing Sunset and Waimea, and he gets a call from his brother Dave, who says, 'You're not gonna believe what we have in our backyard.'"

Richard Schmidt remembers that for the rest of the conversation, he could barely get a word in. His brother told him, "You can drive semi trucks through these barrels!" and proceeded to foam at the mouth attempting to describe the heaviness of Maverick's. But what really got Richard's attention was Dave's admonition to him about his return from Hawaii: "Bring your big guns."

A "gun," to a surfer, is a board. Generally speaking, the

taller and more energized a wave becomes, the longer a surfer's board needs to be in order to allow him to safely make the drop down the face, get to the bottom, and have a chance to navigate the barrel itself. Until that day in 1990, most Californians would surf even the larger waves in their region on boards of eight feet or shorter. Dave was telling Richard Schmidt he'd need his Hawaii-sized board, something well in excess of nine feet and probably closer to ten, if he wanted to attempt the spot off Pillar Point in his backyard.

Not long after that, Richard Schmidt began surfing Maverick's, and it was his benediction upon the place that seemed to throw open a wider window of acceptance. "He had a lifetime of big waves," Jenkins says. "When he came back and said, 'This crushes Steamer Lane; this is legitimate; this is as heavy as anything I've ever seen in Hawaii,' then these other guys knew that they weren't seeing things. It really was what it appeared to be." A photo of the spot, taken by Steve Tadin on a day when Mavs was absolutely going off, was published in *Surfer* magazine later that year and confirmed the finding. Jeff Clark hadn't been hallucinating. He had not been wrong. All Clark had been, really, was ahead of the curve.

Paddling out for extended sessions with Clark, Santa Cruz legend Vince Collier, and the others who would comprise the first real "crew" to surf Maverick's in the early 1990s, Richard Schmidt gradually became convinced of one thing: people were going to die there. The way feckless newcomers attempted to navigate the drop made him cringe. Surfers were switching back and forth between boards shorter than eight feet and as long as ten, and many of them were subsequently getting crushed because of lousy decisions. It was obvious that no one but Clark had yet put enough time in at Maverick's to really know how to approach the wave from day to day. Only Jeff, with his sense and intuition about the wave honed by years of quiet observation, seemed consistently prepared to meet the point as it came.

Fate chose well with Clark when it came to Maverick's. Far from being diffident to out-of-towners, he evinced a spirit of celebration whenever someone new joined the crew. For all of Clark's sense of himself as the Magellan of Mavs, he was remarkably welcoming, even helpful. Everything he knew about the ocean, its time and tides, told Jeff that the spot wasn't really his in any grand sense. At his core, Clark was happiest on the water, connecting with the wave. That others wanted to feel the same connection didn't bother him, it energized him—and he didn't spend too much time worrying about being overrun by kooks. The fakers and wannabes would never make it past a session or two at Maverick's, anyway; the wave had its own way of sorting the wheat from the chaff. If the best big-wavers in the world wanted to come take their hacks, so much the better. Clark was never beyond the idea of learning something from the recognized masters.

Considering all that is known about the place today, one of the fascinating elements of Clark's unique relationship with Maverick's is the fact that, at first, he saw only half of it. From where Clark was hunkered down day after day, either on the hillside at Half Moon Bay High or on the bluff southeast of the surf point itself, the Maverick's wave appeared to break left—that is, the great force of the wave looked to break eastward, toward the northwest edge of the bluff. That's the essential view from the side, but it's only partial. In its full glory, and viewed straight on, the wave actually breaks both left and right. It is the majestic right-breaking face that is most often ridden and produces the most dramatic, intensely violent photographs of surfers either descending the gargantuan wave face or being dumped into the icy wash. But Clark saw the left break first, and that was a good thing. The left helped Clark believe he could find a way to surf it.

Clark's natural position on a surfboard as a teenager was the opposite of what is considered standard. Of his own volition, he stood with his right foot forward on the board and his left behind—"goofy-footed," in the parlance. Most surfers, usually in line with their handedness, keep the left foot forward and use their right to dig the board's fin into the water and set the rails at the desired angle and direction. A so-called regular-foot surfer favors a right-breaking wave, so that his body is facing the tube and he can see what's happening and on what scale as the wave breaks. A left is out of the question for most save the advanced "regular-foot" surfers.

When Clark saw the left at Maverick's, he realized he could handle it because his goofy-foot style meant he could face the wave. Where his friends foresaw broken bones and concussions from not being able to read the grinder accurately as it crashed down around them, Clark saw the opportunity for an amazing ride. Clark got the waves and he rode them well. By following him out there, some of the greatest surfers in modern history slowly began to see how to ride Maverick's and survive it, and eventually how to surf it and love it. You had to be willing to accept the caveats: it was damned cold, it was complicated, and if something went wrong, it had a chance to go very wrong. As Clark reiterated several times, before anyone paddled out to Maverick's, it was incumbent on the surfer to decide whether he was prepared to deal with the worst-case scenario.

But even as years passed and more and more people came in search of the wave, when Clark looked oceanward he almost never saw danger or darkness. When he looked at Mavs, he saw the thing that he wanted most in his life, possibly the thing he needed the most in his life. He needed the connection. "You feel small," he said, sitting in one of the chairs set facing due west off the deck outside his condo. "That's part of it. You feel your place in the universe when you're out there on that wave, that you are a small part of something much bigger. And that's why a lot of us surf in the first place."

To Jeff, the days were all good. He was the leader of the expedition. He "showed" other people the most fantastic surf point in California, the one that had been sitting there for hundreds or thousands of years, waiting to be discovered. He was the first one to the mountaintop, Hillary himself. It was years before Clark would decide he wanted to take the whole enterprise a step further. Which means it was years before the weirdness really began to set in.

Chapter 4

HE WAVE HAD BEEN COMING FROM way off in the distance. Chris saw it. In that sense, it was no surprise. He saw it forming out on the horizon, where it looked so far away and so slow in building that he figured he would have no chance to ride it. It would slide underneath him as it continued to gather momentum toward the shoreline. He understood that he needed another wave soon. Another ride would let him score enough points to advance out of the contest's first round. But this wasn't going to be it. Chris was already paddling so far out that it seemed impossible the wave would break in time for him to catch it. It was his biggest miscalculation.

Up until that point, Bertish's day had felt like a win on every level. He was in one piece. He was in California, not stuck in layover hell in Detroit or still trying to hop a flight out of South Africa. He had arrived missing his stuff, it was true; and he was without his favorite big gun on the planet. He was running on a couple of hours' rest, his body clock still attuned to Cape Town, from which he had embarked on his thirty-six-hour travel "day" through the byzantine world of airlines and their unique concept of baggage handling. He had left South Africa with a board and a wetsuit—nothing else, neither a toothbrush nor a razor. He made it to the U.S. with only the wetsuit. No matter. Chris had left almost on a dare, but certainly on a journey of conviction and hope. The hope remained, and, thus, the conviction—and Bertish was in the water, on contest day, at Maverick's.

The waiting had been the most agonizing thing. Even by the standards of a person who spent his life riding big waves, which seldom break anywhere with predictability or regularity, the last two years at Maverick's had been a test of his patience. Anybody could see that the contest had gotten screwed up. And after the infighting that accompanied it, the surfers themselves had begun either to suffer or grow indifferent. If the organizers couldn't come up with a decent event, then the riders would go on doing what they normally do, which was to surf the wave with enthusiasm and with nothing "official" riding on it. But Chris wanted more.

For a decade, since the first time that Jeff Clark announced his intention to gather the world's greatest big-wave riders for a contest, Bertish had longed to find himself in the lineup. At the time, nobody around Maverick's had the slightest idea who he was. He was chasing waves all over the place, slowly establishing himself among the big riders in the world. Year after year, he found a way to get to Half Moon Bay, in the hope that Clark would recognize his ability and dedication and find him a spot. But year after year, the field was littered with talented riders. As good as he was, as obviously as the spirit of Mavs was deep in his heart, Bertish just had to wait his turn.

It finally arrived in the 2008–09 season, when Jeff added Chris to the list of The 24—just about the ultimate tribute in big-wave surfing. His selection set up Chris for a storybook winter. Instead, the year passed like a cruel hoax. Bertish had hopped a flight to get to Northern California and surf the area, waiting for the contest to be called, and even on the limited time budget of a man leaving his business in South Africa he had enough days to make something great happen. But those days ticked by, one after the other, with nothing to show for them. Maverick's was flat and glassy. The boys came and went, dropping in from all over the world for a few days or weeks at a time in the hope that the point would deliver a great swell; but with each passing interval, it became more and more apparent that conditions were unfavorable, perhaps historically so.

And when greatness finally did unfold itself, on an epic Thanksgiving weekend of massive surf, the idea of the contest itself came and went. Beyond the obvious snag that it was a holiday weekend, the organizers simply weren't in place yet to run the thing. The sponsors weren't lined up. The money wasn't there. And so the contest window hadn't been officially opened. There was nothing yet with which to pay for any of the services that might be rendered. And that weekend of huge surf proved to be an anomaly in an otherwise miserable,

La Niña–induced, low-surf winter. Chris Bertish sat around drinking coffee at Jeff's condo and surfing lousy conditions simply because he was already in town. It was a total loss.

By the next winter, Bertish had made his decision: if the Maverick's contest didn't go off again in 2009–10, he was through. He had carried the torch for a decade and blown through most of his savings to constantly show up in California in addition to the other places he wanted to surf, and if it wasn't going to happen now, the hell with it. The same twenty-four riders from the failed '08–'09 winter season were carried over to the next contest, so Chris was already in. Keir Beadling, the CEO of Mavericks Surf Ventures and Jeff Clark's business partner, had announced that the money from last year's prize purse was going to be rolled to this year's contest, so the window of opportunity for the event could be opened on November 1 for the first time in recent memory. All of the locals agreed that November and December routinely produced great days, contestable days; the organizers simply hadn't been ready that quickly in the past. This time, everything was in place. The only thing left was to pray for a storm to pass through the eye of that needle and get to Half Moon Bay.

The requirements for a contestable day were incredibly strict: waves of at least 40 feet, preferably, with little or no wind, and particularly none of the offshore variety. Those conditions had to appear early in the morning and hold up most of the day in order to surf the four first heats, the two semifinals, and the final. Given such a list, contest organizers and the surfers themselves needed every possible available day of the winter surf season in order to grab one of the perhaps ten or twelve such sessions that might ultimately materialize.

Chris again took no chances, only this time he knew he was close to the end. He bought a ticket to San Francisco to be there when the window opened in November; he planned to stay until New Year's, and after that he knew he would have to head to Cape Town and get back to the everyday work of calling on clients and repping the surf brands who came to his company looking for exposure and sales. But there was room for hope. For starters, everyone knew of the incredible forecast for the winter surf season. It set up as an El Niño season, with conditions in the North Pacific creating storm after storm, which would produce swell after swell that pulsed out on the long journey toward the West Coast of the United States. Odds were that some of those swells would eventually create the killer waves for which Maverick's was known, and it was going to start early this winter. It had a chance to get great and stay great, and the surfers agreed that, after the terrible winter of 2008–09, they had one coming. Bertish wasn't missing it.

But Maverick's wasn't finished taunting Chris. For two and a half months, huge days on the water blew past without a contest. In the meantime, the long-running, behind-the-scenes sparring between Jeff Clark and Keir Beadling over the direction of the contest had finally splashed into the surfers' lives. Over the previous summer, Clark had been deposed as contest director, and he subsequently resigned from the board of Mavericks Surf Ventures, the company he had co-founded with Beadling. Jeff's abrupt departure left the twenty-four surfers to call the contest themselves, relying on a network of e-mail exchanges, texts, and a few cell phone calls to debate whether a particular day could be green-lighted for the event. A majority vote was needed to go. To Chris, it felt like barely controlled frenzy.

In public, in communications with local media, Beadling portrayed the decision to remove Jeff as a release from the "tyranny" of the contest being decided by one man. Many of the surfers, though, had said they would gladly entrust Jeff Clark with that decision every year, just as they had done for a decade. Few had any reservations about Jeff making the call to conduct the event, and if the contest day turned out to be something short of classic, others were content to let Clark bear the responsibility. His batting average was terrifically high, anyway. He had overridden the doubts of some of the people he regularly consulted, including his friend Mark Sponsler, and called the 2008 contest that Greg Long won, which turned out to be a perfect day. He did the same in 2006, the year that Twiggy shocked the big-wave world with his Mavs performance. Neither of those contests would have been run based strictly on wave forecasts or weather models; instead, Clark came up with the right decision by relying on his own sense of Maverick's and other intangibles of the day.

Just as significantly, Clark had refused to call a contest in 2007, because none of the days that were allotted within MSV's abbreviated "window" came close to fitting his criteria for a true competition day at the break. The 2008–09 season had been more of the same, despite a growing sense of desperation for an event. Beadling's company needed a contest run for the business model to gain some traction, and although Keir still ultimately deferred to Clark, he had pushed Jeff to consider days that, deep down, Jeff knew had no chance.

Clark was fighting on more than one front that winter of 2009. Every day was for him spent in pain, sometimes searing pain. The years of constant pounding had ravaged him physically. Among some serious everyday aches, he also needed a complete resurfacing of one hip, a procedure that was going to keep him out of the water for a month and a half or longer. It was an unbearable thought to a man who practically lived on the ocean, but Jeff had reached a point at which even standing up on a surfboard could throw him into agonized spasms. He had stopped surfing left breaks because of the pain that the stance on his board caused him. Some of the surfers believed that, for the first time they could remember, Jeff actually might have entertained the notion of calling the contest on a somewhat lesser day, just to get the thing over with so he could go to the hospital and start getting some relief. But in the end, Jeff couldn't do it. He would not schedule his beloved event unless the right day came along. It didn't. Months later, Jeff was out as contest director.

Now, in the 2009–10 season, the process of calling the contest had fallen into an almost open interpretation of who was in charge, and Beadling was asking the surfers to do the deed themselves. They had vast resources of information and a ton of local knowledge—Washburn, Peter Mel, Kenny "Skindog" Collins—that could be brought to bear, but it was difficult to lock down a date without a captain to make an official decision. An early November opportunity fizzled when great wave conditions were overridden by concerns about off-shore winds that would chop up the surf. Worse, some of the most tantalizing days of those first two months fell victim to the holiday blackout periods—Thanksgiving and Christmas weeks, when the waves were huge but not enough of the out-of-area surfers could even attempt to get to Half Moon Bay to ride them.

By early January 2010, Chris Bertish had had enough. He had surfed Mavs for another year and enjoyed some wonderful rides. There had been good days on the water and good evenings with friends. But all in all, it was another loss. He had come across the world for a contest that just refused to happen. His time was up, his disgust level was high, and the thing he had been chasing for ten years remained only a vision in his mind. He had to go home. He got on a plane, made the forever journey back to Cape Town. A few hours after touchdown, bleary-eyed and upside-down on his body clock, he was back to calling on clients. It felt like the end of the road. Remarkably, it wasn't.

Three times over the next three weeks, Bertish found himself rushing toward the airport, engaged in furious e-mail and text exchanges with the other surfers as they pondered whether to call the contest. Going through the motions, hurriedly throwing things into a carry-on bag, keeping his board and wetsuit nearby in case he suddenly needed to catch a flight, Chris realized that he hadn't let it go—that he couldn't let it go, not yet. No matter what he told himself, he still was driven to be in California . What could he say? The thing had its hooks in him.

Chris was completely out of options and unwilling to fake it. During that first set of discussions with his fellow big-wave riders, he borrowed 13,000 rand—about $1,850—from his brother and set up a ticket to San Francisco International Airport. Every time he subsequently changed a date on the outbound or return flight, it cost him another thousand rand, but Chris decided not to let debt guide his decision. He was in so deep that he'd be spending the next few years trying to pay people back, anyway. It was only money. He wanted to get on the plane.

Two false starts came and went. Finally, on February 11, Bertish read through a series of increasingly urgent e-mails, and the information he found was the stuff he had been waiting for all winter. The storm pattern was solid. The swells were promising. The weather at the surf point itself was somewhat cooperative. The wind off Pillar Point no one could predict with certainty, but all the other signs were there to suggest that the waves could be huge, perhaps the biggest in the history of the contest. And so, at about eleven o'clock at night, Bertish laid down the extra ticket-change money—this time he borrowed the difference from a friend—and bought a seat to the United States. It was surf Maverick's or bust, for the very last time. And now Chris sent an e-mail of his own. Screw rationality and the vagaries of offshore winds, he told Keir and the surfers. If no one else had the guts to call the event, then Bertish would call it all the way from Cape Town. "I'll see you on Saturday—at Mavericks," he wrote. With that, he pushed Send and boarded the plane. What he didn't know was the manner of adventure that lay ahead.

Bertish got as far as Detroit, Michigan, before the trucks started coming off. Waitlisted through his entire itinerary, he had been lucky to get a seat on the plane leaving Cape Town International, and lucky again on his first connecting flight out of Amsterdam. Now, in Wayne County, fortune spat on his shoes: there was no room for him on the connecting flight to San Francisco.

"Please," Bertish begged. He felt a small panic rising inside him. If he missed this flight, nothing else would get him to SFO in time to reach Half Moon Bay before the contest began.

"You'll have to wait like everybody else," the airline official replied. She didn't appear terribly inclined to make an extra effort.

Bertish laid on the syrup. It was all he had left. He started explaining all about the event. He reminded the woman about Tom Hanks in the movie *The Terminal*, and said that he might well find a similar fate right there in Detroit, stuck in the airport forever—that was how broke he was. He made sad eyes. He begged some more. He stood right there at the counter, waiting for a miracle to be delivered. He smiled and joked. He turned up the South African accent that Americans find vaguely exotic. And, however miraculously, in the eleventh hour and fifty-ninth minute, the airline official suddenly found him a seat, a spot normally reserved for flight attendants deadheading to other assignments. Chris rushed aboard before anyone had a change of heart. He was traveling so light that he didn't have to worry about finding a place to store his things. Anyway, the only item he truly had to have, his nine-foot one-inch Jeff Clark original surfboard, was something he'd been forced to check with the other luggage.

Hours later, standing in the SFO baggage claim area, Chris Bertish waited for that one piece of checked baggage, his surfboard. He waited some more, watching the carousel go round and round. The travelers around him gradually collected their things and left. Finally, after all the other people on his flight from Detroit had gone, Chris looked at the big, empty carousel, and he made the slow, lonely walk over to another airline employee, to ask the question he didn't want to ask.

"Oh, that happens," the employee said. "Sometimes luggage doesn't make the connecting flight on the international trips. I'm sure it'll be here in a day or two."

"But I'm in an international surfing event tomorrow," Bertish replied.

The man brightened. "Don't worry! You can rent a board at the beach."

Chris stepped back from the counter and considered everything. He took a few deep breaths. The facts, once he laid them out, weren't entirely horrific, the current unpleasantness notwithstanding. He had made it this far, which already beat the odds. He was in the Bay Area with hours to spare. Screaming at a baggage clerk at midnight, when Chris knew full well that his surfboard was either lost to the ages or a few days away from seeing any part of the West Coast, probably had the least chance of helping him get anything he really needed.

Besides, Bertish had a better option.

• • •

WHEN CHRIS WALKED OUT into the clammy night air in front of the terminal, Jeff Clark was waiting for him. On the night before the contest that Clark created, the one over which he no longer exerted any official control, Jeff was running a taxi service for his friend—exactly the kind of support that those who knew Clark would expect from the person who put the Maverick's experience together in the first place.

Chris and Jeff had bonded a few years before, and again when Chris spent time at Jeff's place during the failed contest season of 2009. In addition to his basic respect for what Jeff had started at Maverick's, Chris trusted Jeff's judgment on the type of board he should be using, and he wanted Jeff to build and shape his big guns for him. He sat with Jeff for hours, listening to Clark spin stories about the surf point—about points all up and down the North Coast, for that matter—and Chris had come to learn what most of Jeff's local friends already knew: every tale, no matter how large, had a ring of truth. Clark had surfed amazing spots, endured incredible wipeouts, stood tall with the giants of the industry, gone it alone on days when no one else would even approach the water. If he said it about the surf, he meant it. On the ocean, on a board, Clark was the real deal.

"He's part Neanderthal," a friend said. "I'm telling you, those knuckles are made of granite. Just because he survives a wipeout on the rocks doesn't mean you're going to survive a wipeout on the rocks. He's not the same as you. That's the first thing you have to understand about even considering trying to do the stuff Jeff does. He's built differently than other people, inside and out. It causes him all sorts of trouble on dry land, but in the water, forget about it."

Many of the surfers, and most of the people who had come to spend time around Maverick's and the contest, regarded Jeff Clark with a sort of ambivalence born from experience. First and foremost, there was respect. When it came to the surf spot itself, there really was no more valuable contact on the face of the earth. If you wanted to know about the wave, how it broke, how to approach it without getting killed, how to be awed by it and still have an incredible time out there, then Jeff was the man. He was generous in ways that were difficult to even calculate. He shared his knowledge of the wave and greeted newcomers with only a slight bit of suspicion, and he was ready to celebrate a great ride with just about anybody who caught one.

Clark's feel for the surf, and the longing he had to be connected to its natural force, came ringing through in every session he shared with other riders. It was a deeply attractive quality that, in its own way, was at the heart of his business. His ramshackle little storefront over on Harvard, opened in 1995, actually belied the growing nature of his enterprise. Clark's reputation as the godfather of Maverick's had done nothing to hurt his standing as a creator and shaper of all types of boards; despite the humble look of the building into which people of all sorts found themselves wandering, to take a photo with Jeff or buy a T-shirt, the truth was that Clark was busy enough to have set up a separate production facility down near San Diego in the mid-2000s. He retreated there often, spending days at a time cutting down huge pieces of foam into recognizable board figures, then shaping them to the customized dimensions of his clients. At times he worked until the foam shavings covered the entire shop floor and left him standing in a mock shallow-water wash. It was by no means a huge-money business, but the work was steady.

Beyond that, Clark was always in demand to be the star of what might be called the Jeff Clark Show, in which he told stories for visitors, signed their books and hoodies and boards and anything else they wanted signed, and perhaps sold them a little something on their way out the door. It was that part of the Clark persona, the walking around and shaking-hands part, for which Mavericks Surf Ventures and its CEO, Keir Beadling, had for years paid him very handsomely.

No one in the water begrudged Clark his renown; he came by it honestly. He was the one who had surfed the place alone for fifteen years. He was the one who had introduced Mavs to the rest of the world. He shared what he had found with some fellow big-wave riders to whom he couldn't wait to show the place, all in the name of having a great day on the water. He had repeatedly taken the worst beatings that Mavs had to offer, and he had popped up to the surface again every single time. He knew so much about the break that he could surf it in any conditions, at any time, with anyone. If Clark decided that a given day was too dangerous out there, that was simply the end of the conversation, because if Jeff wouldn't surf it, then the wave could not be surfed. If anybody deserved to be famously associated with Maverick's, by rights it was Jeff.

Beadling was, for the longest time, appropriately wary of alienating Clark despite the growing differences between them about the future of the contest and the company they shared. Keir knew that most of the world associated Maverick's with only one man, if they knew the place at all. Jeff's story was legend among the surf crowd, and that story was a significant ingredient in the Mavericks Surf Ventures growth plan. The best thing that could happen for the company, in terms of how it would be viewed publicly, was for Jeff to be the public face—giving the interviews, being photographed, showing up for the exhibits and surf-movie screenings, all of that. There was no upside, to the stockholders of MSV, in seeing Jeff Clark diminished in any way.

Privately, those who knew Beadling said he was growing troubled by Jeff's unwillingness to toe the company line and by his ineffectiveness as part of the Mavericks Surf Ventures board of directors. Clark still operated on a surfer's schedule, and he could go underground for long periods of time when a phone call might be needed to deal with a company issue. From Keir's perspective, MSV was paying Jeff pretty good money to be a living example for the company, and all Jeff had to put forth beyond that was some basic cooperation. Instead, it was clear to those who knew both men well that Keir and Jeff were temperamentally unsuited to each other as business partners. They approached their lives almost from opposite ends of the telescope, and Keir's business-first mentality was strikingly dissimilar to Jeff's guiding notion of living for the day.

But that was all behind the scenes. Clark saved his caustic thoughts about Beadling for longtime surf buddies and friends, and Keir had long since made up his mind that what-ever he felt about Clark was best left submerged altogether. He had no interest in tearing down his own building.

"Sometimes, when a person is learning about our company for the first time and they don't know Jeff, they'll say, 'Wow, Jeff has a huge stake in your company. He's your largest share-holder,'" Beadling said during one of a series of interviews he granted for this book. "But the thing is, we wouldn't even be having this conversation but for Jeff. He's the one who went out there for fifteen years by himself. So yes, there are trials and tribulations, but you're working with a guy who is incred-ibly gifted and talented."

Clark's solid reputation among the surfers was rooted in who he really was when it came to the other guys in the water. Clark was exactly the kind of person who would turn over the guest room in his condo (or the couch, or the living-room floor) to a friend who needed a place to stay. First-time visitors were occasionally instructed to bring coffee, but other than that, Clark's place was essentially a 24/7/365 hosting center. Avenue Balboa, a street graced by the tall trees planted in the greenbelt park behind it, sat up in Granada above Princeton, a kind of sentry to the harbor and the water below. It was the nerve center of almost all the significant activity that occurred with regard to Maverick's as a surf point or a contest destina-tion. Jeff often stood in the living room and made his calls and texts, burning up the keypad on his cell phone while reaching out to the opinion leaders of the big-wave community: Greg Long, Twiggy, Pete Mel, Washburn, and the like. It was at one of his barstool seats that Clark sometimes sat for his conversations with Keir, who was at MSV's offices in San Francisco. During one such call, Clark held the phone out so that guests could hear Beadling telling him that the contest no longer could simply be called on twenty-four hours' notice or, say, moved back to Sunday if Saturday didn't turn out to be the day everyone imagined it might. The "one-day" proclamation would continue to be issued for purposes of publicity, but the reality was that the entire operation needed to begin massing several days before the actual contest, so that the personnel and service providers and such could then pounce within a day or two of the event being officially green-lighted. It made sense when applied to the scale of the Maverick's operation, but that didn't stop Clark from treating the call as an incoming hostility.

But that was Jeff. His friends knew this by now; it was part of the light-side, dark-side personality that Jeff sometimes carried through days and weeks. His amusement or irritation at whatever was happening in front of him was readily apparent to anyone who walked by. If you were to get to know him, he would almost immediately find a way to make you comfortable, and that usually would entail him simply going ahead and living out loud. Sometimes, that meant loudly unhappy. Jeff was in almost every respect a genuine person, but when it came to his life on dry land, Clark also could be an enigmatic figure, one who was known to complain about the business that he was a part of. Even those very close to him said they sometimes struggled to understand what he wanted, or what would make him happy.

He had his surf shop, a thing he organized and ran in ways

designed specifically to allow him to close the doors—or leave the storefront to his workers—when the surf was right or the golf conditions too inviting to ignore. He had all but founded Maverick's as a big-wave site. It was Jeff's idea to collect the supreme riders from all over and put them in the water on the same day for a contest that might determine, unofficially, the best big-wave surfer on the planet. Jeff was the unelected mayor of the surf point, the biggest badass connected with one of the roughest waves in God's creation. It was a rare and incredible thing. It seemed as though it should be enough.

Chapter 5

W HEN JEFF MET KEIR BEADLING IN May 2003, what transpired was the seminal event in the creation of the monster that became the current Maverick's Surf Contest. Beadling was a Bay Area sports promoter and entrepreneur, a bright young lawyer who a few years earlier had quit his job as a large-firm litigator—this, Beadling said, after a moment of clarity in which he realized that almost everything he was truly interested in took place outside. He founded a company, Evolve Sports Management, which was primarily searching for sponsor-attractive athletes in emerging sports like surfing, skating and snowboarding, and early on he landed a name client in ultra-marathoner Dean Karnazes. One day a business outreach led Keir to chat with a professional triathlete. The triathlete knew another multi-sport competitor familiar with Jeff Clark's circles, who in turn suggested that Clark might welcome a meeting. Keir wasted no time in setting up a get-together at a coffee shop. It was a humble enough beginning.

By the time he sat down with Beadling, Clark's frustration with trying to make Maverick's something more than the surf point he had "discovered" was beginning to build. After coming up with the idea to inaugurate the contest in 1998, he managed to bring in Quiksilver as a corporate sponsor, and the event was originally titled the Quiksilver "Men Who Ride Mountains" contest. The two sides squeezed out two events, in 1999 and again in 2000, with Santa Cruz mad bomber Darryl "Flea" Virostko winning both of them and each contest getting a warm reception. But in the winter of 2001, the relationship took a hit. A near-perfect swell was advancing on Maverick's from the Pacific, but Quiksilver officials balked at calling the contest. Another big-wave event that the company sponsored, the In Memory of Eddie Aikau competition at Waimea bay in Hawaii, had just been run a few days earlier, and the home office didn't like the idea of so much promotional overlap. Ideally, they wanted five or six weeks between contests. Not only that, but several of the top surfers, including some who were sponsored by Quiksilver, had already made plans to explore the remote Cortes Bank surf reef nearly 100 miles off the coast of Southern California. The company simply couldn't let Maverick's go off without getting the bang for the buck that it thought it was paying for.

Thus, the great weekend at Pillar Point came and went with scores of tremendous rides but no contest. And, remarkably, that was that. Quiksilver soon bolted from Half Moon Bay and Jeff Clark, opting to take up permanent residence at the warm, welcoming Eddie, an event it continues to sponsor today. Jeff was left holding a cold-water, winter-month event that he had never organized by himself, at a cost he couldn't begin to cover, with logistics that no one person could handle. The Maverick's big-wave contest went dark for three years.

It was during that interim, years in which the point was surfed with ever-increasing intensity and renown, that Maverick's began to take off, both as a destination and as a media sensation. Clark's early, lonely years there were a thing of the past. Jeff himself was very much a part of the Mavs story of the present, but he was slowly becoming a touchstone interview subject, a resident sage about the place whose anecdotes were being mined by the local and national press. Jeff had always been generous with his time, but was he supposed to give away all of his experience and knowledge for free?

Not only that, but other people were beginning to put their professional marks on Maverick's. A gifted San Francisco writer and surfer, Matt Warshaw, put together a book about the formative years of the place, *Mavericks: The Story of Big-Wave Surfing*, which included the most in-depth examination of Mark Foo's death ever written. The filmmaker and longtime surfer/skater Stacy Peralta was creating his big-wave documentary *Riding Giants*, a work that would go on to define much of the nature of the movement and become an unofficial film and oral history of the big-wave enterprise worldwide. Though Clark was interviewed at length, figured prominently in the documentary, and was paid for his time (and despite the fact that Maverick's was only one of many places featured), Jeff was left, friends said, with the growing feeling that others were finding ways to profit from a place that he'd gotten to first.

Keir Beadling and Evolve Sports arrived as a lifeline. Beadling's pitch to Jeff was simple: the company would explore ways of promoting Jeff Clark himself, not necessarily the surf point. It seemed a good fit. Clark was a physical presence, an action-oriented athlete; his eloquence was reserved either for riding the wave or talking about it. And while Jeff was very clearly identified with the one surf point, he might have enough name cachet locally to be attractive to advertisers or retailers who were looking for an image for their products. Clark was proud of his own history at Maverick's and intrigued by the possibility of a new business partnership, especially in the wake of the flameout with Quiksilver. Jeff also had people around him saying that it was his time to step up and be recognized and get compensated for who he was with regard to Maverick's, which by now was becoming an all-out international conversation piece. He took the meeting with Keir because he wanted to. Clark was eager to partner up and get going.

At that first meeting, and for a few months thereafter, Keir's attention was focused primarily on finding ways to increase the exposure of Clark himself—Jeff the surfer, Jeff the pioneer, the local. Beadling poked around trying to get a handle on Clark's reputation and see where it might be put to useful effect. But the more he talked with people on the business end of the proposed deals, the more it became apparent that Jeff's story was inseparable from that of Maverick's. Most casual observers made absolutely no distinction between Maverick's and Clark, because most of them had never heard of the place apart from the story about Clark surfing it. A raw, isolated spot that kicked out cold waves that felt like cement when you hit them, a place that was generally inaccessible to the masses and not broadcast-friendly, did not make for great marketing possibilities. It took Jeff's personal story to humanize Maverick's, Keir realized, and thus the two needed to be joined if there was going to be any business to conduct.

The money, whatever amount it might turn out to be, lay in the contest, Keir finally determined. The money was in a one-day event, a celebration of the daring of the surfers and the inspiration of the wave, whose organization and media outreach allowed Jeff's legend and mythology to be retold and perfected. It was like having a sales pitch from nature. But the sales pitch needed a brand to go with it.

"When we first started," Beadling told me, "there was no notion of a Maverick's brand. Jeff was selling T-shirts out of his shop, and he had run the thing into the ground so many times that there wasn't much there. So when we started in '03, the first thing was just to bring contest surfing back to Maverick's and see what happened. That was it. The contest was it. We could try to go out and do local, piddling stuff, but the really big thing was to build something around Maverick's. So we created this company, Mavericks Surf Ventures, and we raised money. That was the whole thing, to begin with."

After the initial meeting, Beadling drew up a one-page presentation that showed the Evolve company and its logo on one side, Jeff and his surf-shop logo on the other. The agreement was to create a joint venture; Clark would own 50 percent, and Keir, via Evolve, would own 50 percent. Both would sit on the board of the company, with others, including San Francisco businessmen Doug Epstein and Mark Dwight, eventually joining them. In the summer of 2003, the men signed the deal to establish Mavericks Surf Ventures; they met at the Beach Chalet restaurant in Ocean Beach, across the street from the water and literally just a few blocks from the homes of Grant Washburn, Mark "Doc" Renneker, and other local surfing giants. Washburn, who by then had come to know Keir a little and Jeff a lot, remembered what he told Beadling in the weeks leading up to the agreement.

"I wanted Keir to be there, to be involved. I was like, 'Yeah, cool,'" said Washburn. "I met with him way before he made the deal and I said, 'You know, Jeff's going to be a hard guy to work with, and that's just the way it is. That's just Jeff. If you're signing up with him, that's the guy you're going to get. Jeff's the guy who went out and rode the wave by himself. He's not normal, because a normal person wouldn't have done that.'

"Keir heard me. But all he said was, 'Oh, it'll be fine.'"

Beadling wasted little time in developing his strategy, and by the fall of that year, it had taken shape. In November, the new company announced the relaunch of the event that would propel its principals forward as a brand, dubbing it the Maverick's Surf Contest. The name was a registered trademark. The event was owned by the company. Jeff Clark, via Keir Beadling, was claiming his surf.

When the contest went off that winter, early in the calendar year 2004, Darryl Virostko picked up where he'd left off three years earlier. Surfing with his usual combination of flair and recklessness, a bravado built on long experience at the surf point and further fueled by alcohol and drug use that wouldn't be revealed for years, Flea plowed into big wave after big wave, took home the trophy, and maintained his status as the only Mavs champion since the inception of the contest. The waves were solid, the day was good, and the crowd was modest but appreciative. The surfing press celebrated the event. From all appearances, the Maverick's competition had regained its footing. And while it was an MSV production, to anyone who drifted by it felt like a Jeff Clark thing. This was precisely as Beadling wanted it. Jeff's name on the door was good for business.

From the start, though, Keir never saw the contest as an end in itself. In those early months, it was the only thing available to him to promote, and it was obvious to him that nothing else could flow from the Maverick's name if the contest wasn't set right for at least a couple of years. But re-establishing the contest was small change compared to Beadling's other goals. He had no aspirations to be a contest organizer; he could hire people for that. Beadling thought of himself as a brand builder; he was there to grow a company. He had no qualms about calling himself an entrepreneur. He did so routinely and without feeling the need to elaborate. He would use other people's money as startup capital and, in exchange, would cut them in for a share of the success.

And at some point, so the vision went, Beadling might be approached by a mega-investor or company intent on buying him out, and he would sell the contest and Mavericks Surf Ventures. Keir had such confidence in Maverick's as a brand and in himself as a promoter that he was already prepared for the time when a buyout offer might arrive. He expected such. His professional life was going to be spent starting companies, taking them to tremendous heights, selling them at whopper profits, and then moving on to the next new thing. Keir was interested in creating an image of his business career as an unbroken series of successful gestures, as F. Scott Fitzgerald might put it. He wanted it to look easy, whether or not it actually was.

Keir and Jeff shared a guarded relationship born of their divergent backgrounds, and for a while it worked. Keir, trim, youthful-looking, confident in conversation, went out and drummed up interest and investors. Jeff mostly stayed down in Half Moon Bay. From where Jeff stood, it shaped up as a pretty low-effort endeavor, since he didn't have to go into the boardroom much or scare up loose change to run the contest. Keir did all that, so Jeff could hang out and be Jeff. What he didn't understand, at least not initially, was that he and Keir weren't pursuing the same goal.

Jeff was interested in finding a way to make his own involvement in Maverick's, and especially the contest, a modestly profitable thing. He wasn't necessarily trying to ride business mountains, and even if he were so inclined, his energy each day flowed in any number of directions—surf, golf, the shop, etc.—before it angled toward the pure business of Mavericks Surf Ventures, LLC. He was more than happy to cash checks, but he wasn't ever going to put the promotional and venture-capital agenda ahead of his basic needs: to get himself on a board, in the water, or on a golf course.

Keir, meanwhile, was moving past Jeff at about 100 miles

per hour. In those early months, Beadling had already begun to plant the seeds of a master plan, which was ultimately to make the surf contest at Maverick's the cornerstone of a much more ambitious campaign. "We would talk about the contest as if it were the only day that anybody really surfed out there," Beadling said, "and then we realized that there was actually a Maverick's brand that could be created here. We started in an incremental way communicating our message back that Maverick's, the brand, was bigger than the contest, rather than the other way around."

Beadling's approach was multipronged, but its originating idea was simple: he wanted the brand to outstrip the surf point. He wanted consumers, when they heard the name Maverick's, to think of any number of things, not just one of the surfers wearing a contest jersey. They could conjure images of a man hiking the crest of a mountain ridge, a snowboarder in midflight, an ultra-marathoner completing another brutal hill course, a surfer standing up to a monster wave. Beadling wanted Maverick's, as a brand, to stand for a state of mind more than any single event. This was Maverick's as a vibe, not a contest or wave. From a certain vantage point it was a solid strategy, one with other marketplace models like The North Face and Patagonia, which did not need to evoke specific locations in order to sell clothing and other gear.

Even back in the early winter of 2004, Keir Beadling knew how he would ultimately measure success in the new venture. The whole thing would be working, in his mind, when he could discontinue the surf contest forever and not lose a single sale. The point wasn't to kill the contest; the point was to have a company so solid that no single element could knock it off its foundation. Beadling envisioned four pillars of the marketing plan: the corporate sponsorships that flowed from identification with the point, initially hooked by the contest; an apparel line that would take off, fueled by a public infatuation with the wave; a flood of media content that could be marketed and sold, like television broadcasts, webcasts, and DVDs; and other live events that Maverick's could put its name on, like concert series. Keir spoke of the future of the company in wistful terms, envisioning a place where, he said, people enjoyed being at MSV each day "to the point that there's not a real line of demarcation between work life and not-work life." And as for himself, Keir at this point was all about the work side. He never stopped looking for the next investor, the next marketing avenue. He wanted to build Maverick's, gloriously succeed with it, and then make it impossible for a larger buyer to resist.

Beadling was unapologetic about his business plan as it related to Maverick's. He was trying to build something. When he signed up Clark as a client and then as a partner, Beadling says, "Intellectual property, we had none. Money, we had none. There was nothing there. When we showed up, prior to that, there was no contest for three years. Even the logo was not a registered trademark." Beadling took care of those details. He got the contest going again. He gathered what intellectual property there was and got it protected. That first year as MSV together was always going to be a struggle financially, and indeed it was: Flea won his title, but there wasn't enough money yet collected to offer him or anyone else a cash prize for risking their necks. Still, the event was up and running. That was more than Clark could say about the previous three winters. This development was greeted somewhat less enthusiastically by a few of the longtime locals, who preferred that the spot remain the true surf secret it once had been. To Keir and to Jeff, though, it was a necessary step to restore the luster of Maverick's and, to Jeff's way of thinking, keep the point where it belonged: on the short list of great big-wave destinations on the planet.

But despite this suggestion of a joined cause between Jeff and Keir, over the next few years a fundamental rift between them began to make itself apparent. Some saw it as an inevitability. Even among his close friends, Jeff was known as someone who could be challenging to work with anywhere besides the water. Keir found that, while Jeff was a valuable marketing asset and an important name to be able to drop during a client negotiation, he could be difficult to pin down and sometimes appeared uninterested in corporate decisions. Still, whatever else happened, Jeff would always have the basic support and respect of the surfers, and that currency was valuable, even critical. Keir needed the surfers to make the contest, which in turn would launch the company. Without Jeff, he couldn't have them.

All in all, Jeff anywhere but on a surfboard tended to be complicated. But the surfers gave him a lot of leeway. Most of them felt that none of Jeff's land-puddles were the result of anything premeditated or malicious. Some of his peers eventually would be awestruck to learn that Jeff was being paid quite well by MSV, but in any tug of war, they would be likely to have Jeff's back. They viewed Jeff's side of the business operation as him saying, "Everybody else is getting money. Why shouldn't I get money?" Many of the surfers agreed that Jeff was within his rights to dig for a profit, if in fact somebody was going to make a profit off Maverick's. So no one opposed his finding a partner like Keir to try to relaunch the contest. They all knew Jeff couldn't get it done by himself.

But as Keir began to truly press his vision for MSV, the strain between the pair became more obvious. The contest itself was back, but it was back under a restricted set of circumstances and conditions. Keir was trying to fund it with investor money, but the cash was slow to materialize. As a result, the contest window in 2005—and again in 2006—had to be pushed back to January while MSV scrambled for funding, thus eliminating from consideration the potentially amazing surf months of November and December. The surfers flocked to the point during those months anyway, of course, but it bothered them—and it bothered Clark—that a contest that aspired to crown the "world's best big-wave rider" might miss peak days in the season simply because the operational machinery wasn't online. As a start-up, the company necessarily functioned day-to-day, using whatever new money it took in to satisfy existing debts. At the same time, Jeff had begun to realize the true scope of Keir's ambitions. Friends said he worried that he was being outmaneuvered even though, by dint of their contract, Jeff was the largest single shareholder in the company and stood to gain the most from its success.

Keir was thinking big. At one point he had the Hard Rock Café incorporated into his plan to pump up Maverick's as a live concert happening. Amazingly, he pulled it off, with the Hard Rock hosting a couple of shows in New York and Florida. But although the association gave Beadling a huge name to throw out when he went trolling for corporate dollars and private equity, Hard Rock went away in 2007, not to return. Beadling got NBC to televise a taped recap of the competition in 2005 and '06, but the network bowed out after that. Fuel TV, a cable channel owned by Fox, took an interest in whatever MSV could piece together and sell as a program, but it was not a company-making kind of deal. Beadling spoke of producing an annual DVD "à la Warren Miller," a reference to the tremendously successful extreme sports filmmaker, but the hard reality was that, depending on the year, there might not be enough money to finance the production of such a thing, much less get it distributed. Practically speaking, Beadling's company needed several hundred thousand dollars per year to run the event successfully and above the waterline.

In the winter of 2006, the surfers found out exactly how tight things were at Mavericks Surf Ventures. In addition to coming up with prize money for the winners—the champion was to receive $30,000 that season—the past contests had always thrown a small check to each of the twenty-four surfers who rode in the heats. It was a given that every one of the guys would surf Maverick's for free (they usually did), but the $500 appearance fee was a good-faith gesture on contest day, particularly aimed at those who were traveling great distances and giving up several days of work in order to attend. It certainly didn't offset the cost of competing, but the surfers had always accepted the stipend with appreciation. In the winter of '06, the checks didn't show up.

After Twiggy's breakthrough victory and the party that followed it that year, the surfers returned home, and Grant Washburn said he began receiving e-mails and texts asking where the money was. Washburn by no means ran the contest, but the surfers rarely communicated directly with Keir. They all knew that Grant spoke with Keir and had done some film work for him, so the surfers came to Grant with their questions as a middleman. Washburn, flummoxed by the situation, assured his buddies that the checks were coming.

"I was saying, 'No, no, I'm sure they're going to be sending the money. They would never do that,'" Washburn remembered. "Then I found out Keir had waived the appearance fee."

Beadling, Washburn said, explained that the decision was "regrettable." But with a $30,000 first prize and a total payout of $55,000 to the six finalists, Keir was clearly conserving his remaining dollars. The problem there was that an appearance fee had been paid in every Maverick's event surfed until that year, and an appearance fee was normally paid at almost any big-wave event on the planet. It highlighted a recurring theme: Beadling wanted to operate outside the box, using his own business models and rewriting the rules if they didn't fit the needs of Mavericks Surf Ventures. But event protocols, which almost every Maverick's surfer knew because most of them surfed all over the world, were fairly consistent from one stop to another, and something as minor as an appearance fee was a given. The contest—not the wave, but the contest—was beginning to take on some unflattering overtones.

For his part, Keir looked past it, dropped the conversation as quickly as possible, and moved on. One day to the next, one week to the next, today's issues notwithstanding, Beadling maintained an unswerving devotion to the future. His conversations were peppered with phrases like "going forward" and "should be profitable" and "synergistic arc." He had canceled the appearance fees because paying them was problematic. That was all. Since the feedback was negative, he most likely would reinstate the payments for the following season—and that, to Beadling, was enough about that. He was out there tracking bigger game, the kind of corporate sponsorship that would someday fatten those appearance fees to levels that actually *would* pay for the surfers' entire trips. If they couldn't see that, it wasn't necessarily their fault, but Keir needed to keep moving.

Sometimes, things didn't get paid on time. Sometimes, vendors went wanting for a while. Sometimes, next year's sponsorship money ended up paying some of this year's bills. Beadling said he paid most everybody else every month before he paid himself—"That was painful at home," he said at one point—and he said checks went to Jeff Clark no matter what, even in the months when he was left with nothing to pay himself. But to Washburn, Pete Mel, and others, it seemed that Keir was having way too much trouble trying to round up support for a concept and an event—the contest—that should have been, in their view, an easy thing to market.

The contrast with Jeff was hard to ignore, too. Whatever else the surfers made of Jeff, the guy would jump off a cliff if it meant catching a wave. Keir, to them, was from the boardroom. The fact that he wore jeans and a Maverick's T-shirt most of the time did not sway their opinion. They figured they knew a businessman when they saw one.

Keir believed in knowing the ending of the story before he began to create it. In a series of interviews, Beadling drew up a vision of the years to come, when Mavericks Surf Ventures would successfully grab market share from billion-dollar giants like Quiksilver and Billabong. It would thrill corporate underwriters with zeppelin rides right over the top of the wave, where CEOs would gawk as the competitors below risked their lives to deliver epic sessions and collect massive payouts. Quite possibly, one of those moneyed types would see the obvious value in trying to wrest control of a company predicated on such an amazing place, such a sensory-overload experience. One of them might want to buy Keir out—and Jeff, too. Jeff, despite his carping, could still wind up rich. Keir was steadfast in refusing to allow any of the day-to-day unpleasantness to detract from this vision. He ran the company as an ongoing enterprise, but also as a vehicle for the great someday that might arrive.

Whatever Beadling thought about a long-range plan for either Jeff Clark or MSV, in the short run the contest was the engine that could power almost everything else. No matter how many times Keir reiterated the company line about the contest only being held if the conditions matched the integrity of the place's history, the reality was that having the contest— every year, if at all possible—was a vital piece. It would be one of the issues that drove Keir's ultimate confrontation with Jeff.

Board intact; surfer missing. First-timers at Maverick's must ponder how much risk they are willing to tolerate before attempting a 40- or 50-foot wave.

Greg Long gets out in front of a massive wall of water off Pillar Point.

Greg Long, one of the most respected big-wave riders in the world, catches a break on the back of a tow-sled.

Grant "Twiggy" Baker and Greg Long, fast friends and members of a tiny subset of sponsored and paid surfers. Baker and Long have traveled the globe in search of the world's biggest waves, usually with a phalanx of photographers in tow.

South African legend Grant "Twiggy" Baker didn't break into big-wave surfing until his mid-thirties.

Paddling into the afternoon sun, Darryl "Flea" Virostko prepares to take on Maverick's once again.

Flea Virostko glances back at the water monster chasing him. Virostko won the first three big-wave competitions ever held at Maverick's.

Grant Washburn, who has probably logged more sessions at the break than anyone over the past decade, throws himself into the maw.

Jeff Clark (left) giving his longtime friend Grant Washburn a ride back out to the wave on competition day. Thrown out of his role as contest director, Clark still found a way to be on the water.

Jeff Clark, godfather of Maverick's, in a moment of pure stoke.

Jeff Clark begins to turn right and surf toward the shoulder of the huge wave about to break upon him. Clark had the rare ability to surf either side of the wave because of his unusual "goofy-foot" stance on the board.

Brazilian Carlos Burle tries to get himself barreled inside a tight break. Burle established himself early on as one of Maverick's gutsiest surfers, taking on waves that others happily let pass.

Carlos Burle won the lasting respect of his peers on contest day 2010 by repeatedly attempting huge waves despite several brutal wipeouts.

Chris Bertish talks things over with a colleague before heading out for another huge-wave session at Maverick's. Bertish arrived on contest day to a chaotic scene on the beach.

Chris Bertish, who arrived at the contest after a thirty-six-hour odyssey from his home in Cape Town, prepares to descend a giant as the wave continues to increase its height behind him.

Chris Bertish tries to outrun an avalanche of whitewash after reaching the base of a wave.

Overhead view of Maverick's as it breaks toward Pillar Point. The surf break is the end of the line for waves that travel thousands of miles from storms formed across open ocean.

The Maverick's surf point. The break at bottom left is where underwater reef-ramps produce waves that often reach heights of 50 and 60 feet on their faces. Surfers and spectators dot the water around the break.

Chapter 6

HE WINTER OF 2007 WAS A GOOD
one for the surf points in Northern
California, or at least a decently
mixed bag. There were quality surf days, a few monster sessions. There were 80-foot waves that couldn't be surfed, and
storms that negated some otherwise golden opportunities. But
because the window for the Maverick's contest again opened
late, most of that was academic in terms of the event itself;
many of the best chances had come and gone by the time Jeff
began tracking the swells with the contest in mind. Keir held
out for a miracle finish. It didn't happen.

Sitting at a North Beach restaurant three years later,
Beadling would say that not having a contest in 2007 was
"one of the best things that happened to the company. It
created some cash-flow challenges, because we didn't get as
many sponsors as we'd like to, we didn't make money the

day of the contest selling merchandise, and all that. But on the other hand, I think it kind of put our money where our mouth was. Yeah, we're a tiny company competing against billion-dollar companies that are producing events in Hawaii and South Africa, but we still have standards—and we're not going to have a contest on a sub-par day." Beadling's reference was direct: just like its forebear, the Eddie Aikau in Waimea, Maverick's was willing to be brutally choosy in order to preserve its heritage.

"It'd be great to have a contest every year," Beadling said. "But not having an event sort of reinforces to your public that this is a special thing, and you really have to have a natural course of events conspire in a perfect way to have an event. I think that when you don't have an event, people realize how special it is."

The words were, as always, perfectly crafted for public consumption. In reality, several of the surfers got the sense— mostly from Jeff talking about it—that Keir was leaning on Jeff to find a way to rationalize green-lighting the contest. Jeff had by then spent three years in partnership with Keir, but this was the first time Jeff's authority over the contest had been brought into question. To Keir it was a straight business move: having the contest was good for everything else that MSV wanted to do, and therefore, in a very roundabout way, it could be argued that it was good for Jeff, the stockholder. But Jeff was first and foremost the self-appointed caretaker of the Maverick's legacy, and he was already annoyed that the contest window was not opened as early as it could have been. Frustrated by the missed opportunity, Jeff adhered to his own policy that he would not call the event if the conditions weren't right. The sub-par swells of the contest period came and went. Jeff made no move. The surfers hung around Half Moon Bay for a while, realized that nothing was likely to happen, and then slowly dispersed. Keir was left to scramble for sponsors and money without an event to market.

By now, sponsor companies were coming and going on a season-by-season basis, with just a few hardy perennials making a constant commitment. And without a 2007 contest to drive new sales, Mavericks Surf Ventures was left with only basic operating capital and a rising set of financial obligations.

Meanwhile, Jeff Clark said he had effectively come to the conclusion, four years into the deal, that partnering with Keir had been a mistake. Whatever Jeff thought he desired by way of the contest or the surf point, it was now clear to him that Keir couldn't provide it through his company. Though friends of his pointed out that Jeff had never had a really firm idea what he wanted when it came to Maverick's, Jeff now said he felt stuck in a contractual agreement that, while attractive enough on the surface, left him feeling answerable to people to whom he didn't especially wish to answer. On top of that, the back and hip issues that eventually would land him on an operating table had begun to assert themselves in the most painful ways, altering Jeff's ability to surf and sometimes severely limiting what he could do on his board. A hint of bitterness began to bleed into his everyday conversation, as if he had somehow been dealt a dirty hand by fate. He mentioned his troubles more often than anyone could remember—rare for Clark, a man willing to endure all manner of hardship on the water.

Most of Jeff's friends and surfing peers, people like Twiggy and Greg Long, reacted to his miseries by commiserating with him on land while trying to get him in the water, the place where he could still find peace. Almost every one of the surfers who knew him well tended to agree that Jeff's psychic wounds were self-inflicted as much as anything else, but they were willing to look past it the way that Clark looked past any special status or standing among those who wanted to try to surf Mavs. Clark's spirit was so welcoming in the water that it bought him a tremendous amount of goodwill. His growing dislike of Keir was going to be a problem for the CEO of Mavericks Surf Ventures for precisely that reason. If he said Keir was a bad guy, the characterization was probably going to stick.

As Clark's and Beadling's relationship frayed, Washburn was caught in the middle. He was loyal to Jeff as a friend but aware of Jeff's mortality on land. At the same time, MSV's struggle to carry over sponsors from year to year placed funding for the contest annually in doubt, and that instability had dire effects on the opening of the contest window, which annoyed the riders. Washburn knew that not only did it make for lousy odds of getting a truly great day, but it was irritating Clark. When in 2006 Beadling compounded the irritation by declining to pay the surfers an appearance fee, Washburn tried to warn him about the fallout.

"I said, 'Hey, you're pissing Jeff off. You pissed off all the surfers,'" Washburn said. "But Keir wants to do everything by himself. He doesn't want to take anyone's word for it."

After the winter of 2006–07 came and went without a contest, Clark called the next season's event just in time for magic to happen. On a clear, cold January day in 2008, Greg Long stuck his perfect ten score on a 40-foot wave face. The contest gained approbation worldwide on the back of the finalists' pre-heat pact to split their winnings equally, which turned the contest into a day devoted to getting great rides instead of skimming money off the next guy. The normally reserved Long capped the feel-good moment when he punched both fists skyward after being crowned the champion. After the dormancy of '06–'07, Maverick's and everything it stood for seemed to be back.

But as the next winter approached and the 2008–09 season loomed, the wheels were beginning to come off. Clark had all but declared open season on Beadling, complaining that Keir was a corporate type who did not share his enthusiasm for the wave or for the point. "He's killing this thing and I can't do anything about it," Clark said at one point. "These guys are just ruining everything. I made a mistake and I can't get out of it yet."

Jeff was, by that time, receiving upward of $12,000 per month from MSV as an independent contractor, according to later official filings. He was paid as both the contest director and all-around brand ambassador. He retained his position as the largest single shareholder in the company, but he was not technically an employee. Keir had structured the deal that way, he said, at Clark's request, because Clark did not want to be employed by MSV. But being on the outside, even with a very decent arrangement, meant that Clark did not have medical coverage through the company, and he knew that he was facing large bills in the near future: his hip had worsened and required the resurfacing procedure if he was going to regain movement and his full surfing life. Despite the income, Clark felt pinched.

Beadling was undaunted, moving ahead. His company had rolled out a Maverick's apparel line, and the maverickssurf.com web site was overloaded with wares for sale. The site once had been devoted almost entirely to the wave and the surfers. Now, on any given day the homepage could bring a new sales pitch; the "news of the day" was often the release of a freshly stocked cap or hoodie or T-shirt. Keir wasn't kidding around. He wanted the apparel line to go viral, then national and international, and finally, fully commercial.

As for the contest, MSV was unquestionably tight on funds. Beadling was trying to raise investor capital and sponsor donations in the midst of the worst economic downturn since the Great Depression. It was almost exactly the wrong time to be asking anyone for money. The contest had been able to slog through the January '08 competition and pay the $30,000 first prize, with a total purse of $75,000, but Beadling needed more. He needed a cash infusion to keep things going, much less improve on them.

The sponsors, big and small, were coming and going. Coca-Cola, which had come on in the early years, left after 2005. Hard Rock left after 2006. Those kinds of international brands offered the best chance to secure serious money, but Beadling also found himself chasing the smaller fish—he needed any capital from any source available. By the time

November 2008 rolled around, the reality was grim. Beadling had interest from several companies, but not the signed documents nor the deposited checks to back it up. There was certainly not enough money on hand to make a dent in the expected outlay for the event. The Maverick's Surf Contest was not ready to go.

For some time, the surfers, the surf media, and Jeff Clark himself had been saying that the contest window needed to open at least by December 1 of each season. More to the point, the Maverick's "winter" really began sometime in October most years, so a true contest window would have been from November 1 until roughly the end of February, perhaps into March. Beadling knew it; he understood what they were saying. He just didn't have the resources to back a contest that early. This season, at least, the contest day was going to have to arrive after the New Year, if at all.

Thanksgiving weekend of 2008 blew in with ferocity. Even the days leading up to it were filled with signs that something huge was about to happen. When those readings finally suggested 20-foot surf and wave faces of 40 feet or higher, the big-wave world and its attendant media descended on Jeff's once-secret spot. It was a spectacle unlike any in the history of Maverick's. Hawaiians Dave Wassel and Mark Healy were rewarded for grabbing quick flights out of Honolulu; they were met at Half Moon Bay by grand barrels and storm-free conditions. Twiggy Baker and Greg Long showed up. Jeff switched off between grabbing his board and operating a watercraft to perform emergency pickups. Nathan Fletcher, Alex Martins, Anthony Tashnick, and most of the truly hardcore locals made the scene. What they got for their efforts were swells that bunched up hard and at brief intervals, less than half a minute between sets.

When Long lost it on the way down one wave, he was plunged under and, unable to find the surface in time, held down by a vicious second wave. Clark sprinted into the foam on his Jet Ski and found Greg, who barely had the energy to grip the sled as Clark got them both out before a third wave broke. Later, Long told his friend, *Surfing* magazine editor Evan Slater, that the force of his wipeout drove him so deep into the bowl that he didn't have a chance to clear his ears before the pressure overcame them. He blew out an eardrum and lost his orientation entirely. "When Jeff tried to grab me," Long told Slater, "I was so out of it that I started swimming straight down."

Conditions Sunday were even more amazing than Saturday, with huge wave faces and brilliant skies. Washburn and Flea Virostko both survived crushing spills that put them on the inside of the reef, where they endured multi-wave poundings before they could get back to safety—yet each man promptly headed back out. The mood in the lineup was ebullient and fraternal despite the overload of people wanting to grab a piece of the action, with surfers loudly cheering each other on and hooting when somebody caught a great ride. Washburn said he couldn't remember a better day, a memory that took him all the way back to the week of Mark Foo's death in December '94, when some of the afternoons had been off the charts. Twiggy surfed both days at full passion and later told Bruce Jenkins, "We are the luckiest organisms in the history of the universe." It was what most of the surfers live for: the moment in which they know, in real time, exactly how good it is. Even among big-wave surfers, such a high is elusive and rare.

In the run-up to the weekend, the proprietors of the Maverick's Surf Contest hadn't been able to even consider playing a role in what turned out to be near-transcendental surf sessions. The full measure of the opportunity that was missed became obvious when Mark Sponsler, the contest's chief wave and weather forecaster, began speaking aloud a certain dread that the best days of the season had just been missed.

What Sponsler knew, or at least what he knew about the winter forecast to come, was that La Niña weather patterns would prevail in the Pacific, producing fewer wave-creating storms and increasing the chances of localized rain at Maverick's itself. A La Niña, for the surfers, was the opposite of an El Niño. An El Niño winter spun out storms seemingly every five minutes; it was more a matter of choosing how often you wanted to go surf incredible waves. A La Niña winter did not entirely preclude great waves—weather never operates on anyone's schedule or in a 100 percent predictable pattern, and storms were still going to be produced out in the Pacific—but the prospects for optimal surf were weak. A whole bunch of stuff was going to have to happen in exactly the right order this winter, Sponsler feared, or most of the big-wave days would be turned to mush by offshore winds or local storm systems. He was right, and it was the weather that helped turn the screws on an already tension-filled situation.

Only a few weeks after the Thanksgiving surf feast,

Beadling nailed down enough principal support to get the contest up and running again. The response from the surf community was understandably muted, considering what had just passed and what could have been. But as it turned out, Keir had a trick left up his sleeve. Not long after the New Year, he stepped up with the stunning announcement that Maverick's was not cutting back, but rather *doubling* its prize purse to $150,000, with a full $50,000 going to the winner. After appearing to founder, the contest suddenly was positioned as the richest payout in the industry.

The angel, kicking in the additional $75,000, was Barracuda Networks, a global Internet security titan based in Silicon Valley whose top executives liked the idea of being associated with a big-wave contest in their backyard. Barracuda had money to spend even in a down economy, and company co-founder Michael Perone didn't want to see the contest struggle right in front of him. Perone's firm had spent scads of money over the years marketing its products via sports, including the Super Bowl, and its investment in Maverick's was minor by comparison. Beadling signed up Barracuda and immediately announced the increased prize purse, with Barracuda joining two equity-firm partners, Moose Guen and Jane Sutherland of MVision, as the major contributors. Maverick's was now, by paycheck, the big dog of big-wave surfing.

For Keir, months and months of scraping around appeared to have paid off in one transcendent moment. In a few weeks the event had gone from life-support to an apparently healthy glow. But there was one significant hitch: there were no waves.

Jeff Clark could see it; there was no question about it. He rose each day to the view of the surf point off his deck, and he could tell with his own eyes what Sponsler's forecasts were already making clear: there were very few storms out there capable of kicking up the conditions that would make great (or even decent) waves at Maverick's. Keir had given the okay to open the contest waiting period, but there were no waves to take the event any farther along the line than that. In fact, the winter of 2009 was shaping up as one of the all-time poorest seasons at Pillar Point.

For Keir and for MSV, it was a worst-case scenario. The integrity of the contest notwithstanding, he'd just lined up a sponsor and had big-time money to award by the standards of surfing. He had the apparel line up and running. He had his plans in place for another crack at a Maverick's Live concert tour, which, when asked about it, he described as something that would attract "the Jack Johnsons and the Ben Harpers and people like that." Beadling had a story to sell right this minute, an inspiring tale about a fledgling company that managed to increase its sponsorship during a recession *and* had a battle plan for retailing that would take its clothing line national and international.

"My whole life is checkers, putting the pieces together," Beadling said over coffee one day. "The checker pieces are much closer to the right side of the board than they ever have been. Now we're working on how you have an asset, how you monetize that. I'm the hunter. I'm the guy who goes in there when it gets to a certain point and who sort of locks it down. Contest or no contest, we're going to have a year-round program, a concert series, TV show running constantly on Fuel, the DVDs. The apparel line should be profitable this year, which is extraordinary."

Beadling could see it all coming together, because his mind worked in that direction. He could always see it all coming together, even when it was nowhere close to doing so. But now, in the winter of 2009, with things actually approaching critical mass, he faced the prospect of no contest to kick-start the other facets of the business. And his partner, Jeff, wasn't about to yield any ground on the only front that could fix it.

As January prepared to give way to February, the pressure on Jeff to call the event became palpable. Beadling was on the phone regularly, wondering about this weather pattern or that swell developing in the Pacific. He was looking for anything, anywhere out there, that might augur contestable conditions. It was plainly grasping at straws and, for what it was worth, most of the surfers were doing the same, only for different reasons: they wanted to surf. But Clark's finely tuned sense of the weather, the wave, and Maverick's as a whole told him that it would take an absolute freak storm to produce anything noteworthy.

Up at the Beach Chalet bar and restaurant in Ocean Beach, Grant Washburn and Twiggy commiserated over the lousy surf, and Twiggy started counting out loud how many days he could afford to hang out. By the end of February, he knew, he would take off; his sponsorship deals, which were all very new, required him to find waves and surf them. If there was nothing going at his current location, he'd better get himself to another spot, and fast. That's what sponsor money was for, to allow him to jump flights quickly, rent a car on a whim, or hire a boat to take him someplace more obscure—whatever it took to find the waves that produced the most dramatic photos and video. Twig and Greg Long were beginning to spend significant travel time together, and they already had gone out on several forays that year. But they always drifted back in the direction of the West Coast of the U.S. in hopes that the contest might magically fall together. Alas, their own eyes—and the days they spent surfing smaller waves around the region—told them all they needed to know about the odds.

"I know the contest window is through March," Twiggy said, "but I can't do it. Can't hang. There is no off-season. I mean, you can't be everywhere all the time, but there is usually someplace that you can go to get great waves. If it's not to be here this year, then it's not to be. Gotta move on."

Sure enough, a few days after that conversation, Twiggy lit out for Ireland, with plans to circle back to Northern California, or Hawaii, or Mexico, or wherever there were waves worth surfing and conditions that made for decent photographs. It was entirely up to the weather patterns now. And that, for Keir Beadling, was exactly the problem.

Chapter 7

EFF WAS DIGGING IN HIS HEELS, clinging to the one thread of control of his own contest that he felt he had left. He was living with severe pain in his hip, he was in a business relationship that he didn't understand and no longer wanted, and he was, as of that moment, in charge of calling a contest that had begun to resemble nothing so much as a giant commercial. But it was still his call to make. And he intended to make it in his traditional way, by sifting through the reams of information, consulting like-minded people who used the spirit of the surfers and the wave as their primary guide, and ultimately arriving at a decision that he could live with. It had always worked. Even the close calls, the times when Jeff chose to green-light the event despite potential weather complications, things had worked in his favor. There had been some greater and lesser days, yes, and the surfers could always wish for something that would have made a certain contest historic rather than really good, but no one could say Jeff had ever made an outright mistake. His decision to go without an event in the winter of 2006–07 had been the right one, too, given the time frame on offer. In this regard, Clark had the confidence of the guys in the water. Someone had to decide. Jeff was the guy.

Now, though, he was fielding calls from Keir more often, calls in which Keir was scrounging for justification to run the event. Keir never betrayed desperation; it was not his style. But the fact that he was calling both Jeff and Grant Washburn, asking about the potential of each middling little squall off the coast of Japan, made his sense of urgency clear. Keir had gone on the record numerous times to say that the call was Jeff's to make, but leaving Jeff to figure out everything by himself made Keir uncomfortable. It was Keir's duty to the company, in his mind, to make sure Jeff understood all the implications of either running or canceling the Maverick's Surf Contest in any given year.

During one of the phone calls, Jeff sat on a barstool in his condo, forming an increasingly exasperated expression while listening to Keir ask about an approaching weather system. Jeff already had spent that the morning talking things over with Sponsler, Washburn, Twiggy, and Greg Long, studying the patterns and the charts. The storm, and the waves it had spun out over the Pacific, just was not enough. Everyone agreed that it wasn't going to happen.

"Well, how long do we have?" interjected Chris Bertish thoughtfully, sitting down at a table across from Clark with a cup of coffee. Though Bertish technically had no control of the contest or its administration, and had never even surfed the event, he used the term "we" with the casual confidence of a person who knew his presence in the conversation was valued. He had no problem offering the question while Jeff was on the phone with Keir.

Clark pondered. Moments earlier, he had heard from Sponsler. "I just don't know what it'll do tomorrow," Sponsler had told him. Mark was ensconced in front of his computer models at his home, studying the swells and sets as they moved across the open ocean toward the Hawaiian Islands. "But I've been looking at it and looking at it, and I don't see it. I don't see what you're going to need."

Clark sank down a little on his stool. If the storm continued to dissipate, which all indications suggested it would, then the waves that reached Half Moon Bay by Friday would be pleasant and perhaps a bit challenging, but nothing in keeping with the tradition. Beyond that, the forecast called for mostly underwhelming surf through mid-February, with March not much better. The contest window closed March 31.

Clark considered his options. His friends were convinced that, although he might never say it out loud, a part of Jeff wanted to relent and call the contest. The sooner he could get the thing over with, the sooner he could get on with getting himself repaired; and the constant haggling over relatively minor waves was beginning to wear him down on every front. The guys on the water had heard enough to know their friend's hurt was real. Jeff was, in many ways, an ultimate competitor; they were used to viewing him as a solid block. And while

Jeff never surfed out of control, he wasn't afraid to charge. It seemed impossible, watching Clark plunge into the surf day after day to take on waves that literally broke other people, that he would ever surrender to the ravages of time. But his hip was just shot. Standing fully upright on his board had become an agonizing experience.

Now, jumping off the phone with Keir and ringing up Twiggy, Clark ran the numbers past Baker, who listened silently for a few moments as Jeff reeled off buoy readings from Hawaii and the wave heights that were being charted there. "That won't be much by the time it gets here, isn't that right?" Baker finally said.

"It's what I'm thinking," Clark replied.

"Have you got another day to wait?"

That was the real issue. In past years, there was always another day, because waiting an extra day just to be sure meant little to a competition that was founded on the idea of short notice. As Clark had conceived the event, part of the allure involved giving the competitors only so much time to make it all happen. Quiksilver, the first sponsor, had loved that aspect of the event—surfers scrambling in from all over in a frantic rush—even though it ultimately tried to manipulate the contest window to suit its own needs. In the MSV/Keir Beadling era, the old "normal" no longer fit. Tons of moving parts had to be coordinated, and there were people to please other than the guys in the wetsuits.

This time, Clark basically asked Keir for an extension. Calling Keir back, Jeff proposed that they wait one more day to make the decision, thus giving the storm a chance to really deliver waves. Beadling understood immediately what was under discussion. It was old school: calling the entire event on one day's notice. Unfortunately, old-school decision-making was not applicable in 2009.

"We can't get everything into place in time," Beadling said. "That's not enough time to do it all. The webcast and all the other things—they take time to get set up, Jeff. The web people have to fly in from Colorado. And the sponsors have to have time to get here so they can see it."

Beadling meant that he needed time to get the contest bankrollers to their event-day tents on the beach, so they could have their drinks and food and watch the action on a big-screen TV. It was pure corporate, the kind of consideration that Keir absolutely had to include in his thinking. Clark crinkled his nose and looked at the friends in his condo with palms upraised, as if to say, "You see? You see what I'm dealing with here?" He might still make the final decision, but so much of the event that he created no longer felt like his. He wanted it to be about the surfers, not the industry.

"Then," he finally told Beadling, "it's a no-go."

"Well, we'll see what it looks like tomorrow," Beadling said.

"Right," Jeff replied. "Tomorrow."

It was just another day, after all. It was just one conversation among dozens. And it would go that way straight down the line. "That's the difference between Maverick's and Dungeons," Twiggy Baker said glumly, referring to the sinister break in South Africa. "Dungeons would never go three months without a really good day." Three months had come and gone since that epic Thanksgiving weekend, and another month would slide by in due time. It was, in Washburn's estimation, the poorest season for waves he had ever seen at Maverick's.

In the end, Jeff stood up for the integrity of the event as he saw it. He gutted out the ensuing days and weeks, took all of Keir's calls. But he would not call a substandard contest, and for anything else that could be said about that winter, the absolute certainty was that from January forward, it didn't come close to producing the type of day that would make a Maverick's event memorable.

The 2008–09 contest window officially closed March 31. The National Oceanic and Atmospheric Administration (NOAA) subsequently refused to grant Beadling a one-month extension to his permit at Pillar Point. The NOAA was particularly concerned about the use of personal watercraft in the area because of the effects of the noise and pollution on the wildlife, and it had made all the exceptions it was prepared to make. It didn't really matter, since the area off Pillar Point was looking like a lake most of the time, with shockingly few surfable days. It was the wrong contest window, for the wrong length of time, with the wrong opening date. Some of those factors couldn't be helped, of course, but even though Keir Beadling had had to scratch and claw for the sponsorships that he did bring in, the reality was that an entire season had been lost. Clark was the only person with enough designated clout to have done anything about that, but he had stayed true to the surfers and their fans. The contest didn't happen on account of lousy stinking waves.

...

DEPENDING ON WHOM YOU asked, Clark's refusal to schedule the '09 event either got him fired or had nothing to do with anything at all. Most of the surfing world subscribed to the former theory. Beadling preferred the latter, and this was both a personal and a legal disposition.

"He's still the largest single shareholder. You can't forget that," Beadling said. At a coffee house in North Beach, a few blocks away from the 900-square-foot office that housed Mavericks Surf Ventures, Keir fiddled with his BlackBerry cell phone, constantly checking messages, and he pondered what his company had done and where things stood. Jeff Clark's "resignation" as director of the Maverick's Surf Contest had been announced a few weeks earlier, in June. In a carefully crafted press release explaining the transaction, Beadling had raised the notion of "democratizing the contest direction process" going forward, and added, "Jeff's legacy is forever etched in the history of Maverick's." It was a well-phrased attempt to minimize the public-relations damage of his decision push Jeff out. It also spared Jeff the ignobility of having to acknowledge that essentially he'd been fired.

But the truth was the truth, and Jeff and Keir knew it better than anyone. Beadling and fellow board member Mark Dwight had removed Clark. Now, sitting at a small table in the middle of Caffe Trieste, Beadling was calculating the damage.

Beadling never would have made the move if he'd thought it meant the end of the contest, or that the decision would trigger a boycott by the twenty-four surfers in the 2009–10 field, the group that was fully carried over from the previous season's no-go. After the announcement, he had taken time to reach out, to explain to key people what was going on and to make sure they all understood that Beadling would have told them ahead of time about the decision if he could have. Keir wanted to shut down any rumblings of dissent as quickly and efficiently as possible. Still, in his final analysis, maintaining the peace was a secondary concern. Priority one was getting the situation with Jeff resolved, and it had resolved like this: Jeff Clark was out.

On some level, Beadling would have liked to tell the surfers and the public all of the reasons why he and Dwight had decided to let Jeff go as contest director. Keir's list might include Jeff's trashing Beadling to people in both casual and public conversation, refusing to carry out responsibilities as a "brand ambassador," being generally uncommunicative, or talking openly about finding a way out of his contract with MSV. However much he might have enjoyed a public airing of grievances, though, Beadling still had the contest to run.

Not only that, MSV had secured commitments from their primary sponsors, Barracuda Networks, Moose Guen and Jane Sutherland of MVision, and Jim Beam bourbon, to roll over all of the contest prize money to the coming season. With those commitments in place, Beadling would be able to open the contest window on November 1, the true start of the season at Maverick's. Meteorologists were predicting an El Niño winter weather pattern, which suggested that swells were going to be firing steadily across the Pacific. Maverick's was likely to provide redline surfing all winter, raising the odds for contest conditions that could outstrip anything yet seen in Half Moon Bay. The company couldn't afford to do anything that might compromise all of that promise.

And so Beadling tried to downplay the reality of what had happened with Jeff. Mavericks Surf Ventures had nothing to gain, but plenty to lose, by a public tarnishing of Jeff Clark's name. "This was not about that," Keir said. "There clearly was no other option. It's safe to say that he was never comfortable, despite our best efforts, in board of directors' meetings, despite the fact that we asked next to nothing of him. It was not his comfort zone." The end had been swift. At a board meeting, a meeting that Jeff phoned in to rather than showing up in person, Beadling and Dwight, the remaining board members, had told Jeff how it was, and that was that.

"I don't know if he was surprised or not," Beadling said, "and it doesn't matter to me if he was surprised or not." In Keir's mind, Jeff's exile would lighten the load on several levels. First and foremost, he wouldn't have to interact with Clark on a daily basis. For some time, Jeff had displayed no interest in MSV's affairs and bristled whenever he spoke with Beadling. He hated the commercial aspects of the venture, even though it was the idea of turning a profit that had lured him to his first meeting with Keir in 2003. But he didn't want to do penance constantly for having sought his own small piece of the action, and as he grew more and more unhappy, he became more and more vocal. Keir found this behavior baffling; he couldn't understand someone taking his money every month and then slapping him around for his trouble. "Anybody in his right mind in that position, getting paid that amount of money, and he's really being asked nothing other than to be himself . . ." Beadling said. He let his voice trail off. No matter now. It was done.

To Keir, the split was simply another thing that needed to happen. He knew that the stakes were higher where Jeff was involved, of course. He had initially built the company around Jeff's image, Jeff's backstory, and Jeff's ability to gather the best surfers in the world regardless of whether the contest was swimming in cash or broke. The first prize was now $50,000, but the surf gods had smiled on Maverick's back when that prize was $30,000, and even before that, when there was no money to be paid. Jeff's name, his international goodwill, and his reputation had made all that possible. Keir knew it reflexively by now. But he also felt that he had built a brand that could withstand anything, even the public disrobing of an icon. He was about to find out.

On a business level, Keir simply couldn't afford for his personal enmity toward Jeff to matter, so in his mind it didn't. That much was an acquired skill. Beadling had for most of his life been a master compartmentalizer, a character trait that emerged when he was fourteen years old and his pregnant mother informed him that she and Keir's father were divorcing.

"I can partition off these things," Beadling said. "I can separate them, and go back to them later. And that's a product of having had my heart broken when I was fourteen. And I would imagine that if there were ever a survey done on professional entrepreneurs, especially serial entrepreneurs, they would probably have that trait, that ability to partition off and compartmentalize."

Still, there was no doubt that what had transpired the previous spring had left a mark. Aspects of Keir's relationship with Jeff had bubbled all the way to the surface, and it was difficult to discern where the personal ended and the business began. The contest was clearly at the center of the conflict, because it was one of the few things over which Jeff had a direct, even massive, influence. His steadfast refusal to call the contest the previous season was Exhibit A. At one point, after passing on that potential January date, he had said, "I want it to be 40-foot faces, and so do the guys. They want it to be very edgy, the best of the best. We don't want a six-foot contest. We want something that will test the mettle of everyone involved in this contest. That's what Maverick's is about."

It was as solid and concise an explanation as any Jeff had ever offered about his hopes for the contest. And for Keir, it was just the purest distillation of the problem. Jeff thought the contest was strictly for the surfers. From a business perspective, he could scarcely have been more wrong.

Other people's input notwithstanding, Jeff said yes or no to having the contest. Jeff decided which surfers were in and which were out. An entire company orbited around these decisions, and although Keir himself was the champion of the idea that, someday, the Maverick's brand would be so powerful that the contest would assume a lesser role, he wasn't there yet. The problem, to Beadling, was that Jeff still thought of himself as "the man of Maverick's," and that attitude wasn't helping the company grow.

Beyond that, Clark had raised eyebrows both within and outside the surf community as he approached the resurfacing

surgery on his hip. The procedure was going to cost somewhere near $60,000. In April 2009, there appeared a web
site explaining Jeff's operation and its cost, promising Jeff's
blogged thoughts as he went through his rehab and slowly
regained the surfing life he loved. It also provided information
for people who wanted to send Jeff money to defray his costs.
The open solicitation struck several people as either awkward
or plain wrong. Jeff's defenders replied that the site was established primarily because people had been asking how they
could help, since they knew Jeff didn't have health insurance.
But Keir knew how much he paid Jeff every year, and Jeff had
his surf shop. Keir tiptoed the line around the subject, not
wanting to come off as unfeeling, but the sequence of events
clearly annoyed him.

Still, it was a minor irritation. The larger issues were the
ones that finally felt irresolvable. "Jeff has done such amazing things, and I admire him as a guy who did what he did,"
Beadling said, pushing a spoon idly around his coffee saucer.
"But Maverick's is also much bigger than one single person.
Everybody recognizes that, for the most part, except for one
person. We wanted to democratize the process. I really feel
that it's fair to say that having the ultimate power as to who's
in and who's out of the contest is dangerous. It was a monar-
chy, and there were a lot of negative aspects to that. And to a
lesser extent, calling the contest in appropriate conditions was
something that shouldn't just be in the hands of one person."

There was overt risk in simply beheading the administration of the contest. Beadling's solution was to appeal to
the surfers themselves. He asked them to consider calling the

contest by group vote, after discussing each opportunity as a collective. Darren Brilhart, a veteran surf contest promoter from Southern California who was respected by the guys and had been brought aboard by them in 2006 as an adviser to the surfers, could provide logistical support on event day and in the weeks leading up to it. Katherine Kelly Clark, Jeff's former wife and a longtime supporter of the contest, was going to stay on in her very general capacity as a micro-organizer to the event and de facto den mother to the surfers, who came to her with many of their needs and questions. Pete Mel, who had assumed the role of elder statesman among his peers, would be a go-to guy for questions about the way things should be done. And although Keir knew that Grant Washburn no longer would work with him, he also recognized that Washburn would be constantly consulted by the other surfers and therefore was central to the success of the new decision-making process. Making sure Grant had access to all the available information on the split with Jeff was critical, because Grant could provide ballast in the court of public opinion. He understood where all the sides were coming from, and he knew Jeff too well to assume it was all one way or the other.

Fortunately for Beadling, the surfers were sufficiently baffled by the events surrounding Jeff's firing that they never came close to organizing a group boycott, or even a serious protest. It wasn't as though they weren't given the opportunity to choose sides. A few days after MSV's official announcement of the change in Clark's status, Jeff fired back with an official statement of his own, and one could almost hear the anger in his words.

"Over the past several years," he wrote, "it has been obvious that my vision and priorities are not in line with those of Mavericks Surf Ventures. I have had in the past, and continue to see, strong differences of opinion with the present CEO and Board about the direction, image and priorities of the company and the contest.

"The press release issued by Mavericks Surf Ventures this week stating that I 'stepped down' and I am 'passing the torch to the next generation' is wrong. The reality is that I was ousted as Contest Director by the current CEO."

Jeff used the news release to announce that he had resigned from the MSV board of directors, an unsurprising development considering the events of the past week, but one that was sure to draw headlines. He reasserted his commitment to "the family of big-wave surfers, the spirit of the ocean, and this amazing wave. I never wanted that to be compromised for the sake of money or marketing opportunities. I think that focus is obvious to anyone who knows me or who has seen my priorities over the years."

Jeff also laid out his worst fear, which was "a committee deciding, based on sponsorship money and media opportunities, when the best day to run the contest would be, and have it turn into just another ten-foot swell with a lot of hype and not a lot of substance." The message was clear enough: Jeff was positioning himself as the noble one. He wanted what was best for the surfers; Keir and MSV wanted their money.

One of the problems with the turn of events, for the surfers, was that Jeff remained the largest shareholder in MSV. He might be off the board of directors, he might be out as contest-caller, but did it really make any sense not to surf, not to compete? Clark stood to gain if the event continued and thrived. As respected longtime local big-waver Zach Wormhoudt told the *San Francisco Chronicle*, "He's been a gracious host to a lot of people over the years, so there's a little bit of a challenge between people wanting to do the contest and wanting to support Jeff. Since there are allegations from both sides, it's hard to know exactly what's what."

For that matter, the surfers couldn't tell what Clark really wanted them to do. On the one hand, Jeff was their guy; his decision not to run Maverick's in two of the previous three seasons attested to that. He wouldn't call the event unless it was going to be true to the spirit of its earliest days. On the other hand, Jeff never advocated a boycott on the part of any of the contestants; and if the guys themselves could all agree on a day that met Jeff's historically tough criteria and go ahead and surf it, wouldn't that be a way of honoring Jeff?

"They're both right, and they're both wrong, and they're forever at odds, and they will never hear each other," Bruce Jenkins had said months before Beadling stripped Clark of his duties. "That's pretty much where all of that lies. Fortunately, that has nothing to do with what goes on in the water. That's probably the saving grace of all of it."

In his own mind, Keir Beadling already was moving on. Whatever the short-term fallout of cutting Jeff Clark loose turned out to be, it was outweighed by the fact that Jeff no longer had any respect for his obligations to the company and its stake-holders. Keir put his faith in Maverick's the brand: the idea that people were already associating Maverick's with a good time, a vibe, a sense of challenge, maybe even simply the image of Twiggy or Greg Long or Flea dive-bombing down the face of a wave—doing the unthinkable, making the impossible come to life. Keir figured that his company had already done the heavy lifting to get the brand out there internationally, to make sure that people knew Maverick's wasn't just a big cold-water wave. He was betting on the web presence and the apparel line and the Twitter account and the concerts and all of it to survive the loss of Jeff.

And anyway, Keir's ultimate bet was on Jeff's absence being temporary. Clark would never be able to let Maverick's come and go without being seen and heard. Employed by MSV or not, paid as "ambassador" or not, Jeff would still be around. More than that, his name would be invoked about every third sentence uttered by anyone who was ever interviewed about the point, and in that way Jeff's spirit and his stoke were still things upon which MSV could capitalize. They didn't need his permission, nor to cut him a check, for that. Jeff was still Maverick's in most of the important ways, and that meant that his image, his likeness, his voice and authority, were already out there in the public domain forever, through the stories and the articles and video archives and in the minds of the surfers who came to be a part of the experience. It would probably be decades before Jeff Clark's shadow even began to move away from Maverick's, if it ever moved at all. By that time, Keir figured, MSV would be fully settled into a rich orbit of its own.

Chapter 8

THE ONE THING THAT GRANT Washburn might not have imagined was seeing himself cast as a referee in the battles that Keir Beadling and Jeff Clark waged on the playing field that was the Maverick's Surf Contest. Then again, there wasn't much about his life as a big-wave surfer that could have been predicted. Washburn grew up in Connecticut, two hours from a beach of any kind, and with his lanky frame he figured primarily as a basketball player, not a surfer. Surfing came by happenstance. Washburn's grandparents had a place at the New Jersey shore, and as a kid he was on a board almost as soon as he saw the friendly beach-break waves—"little foamies," he calls them—rolling gently to shore. No one he knew surfed; no one asked him if he wanted to surf. But he loved the idea of surfing right from the start.

Still, Washburn didn't make it to California until his

twenties, in the early 1990s. After graduating from Trinity College in Hartford, he followed a friend to San Francisco, lured by the promise of $10-per-hour jobs doing architectural remodels around the city. Not long after, a former college roommate arrived, like Washburn a person who had surfing on his mind, and he suggested that the two get a place close to the waves. Sheer luck and availability landed Washburn at Ocean Beach, home of some of the best breakers in the region. There he stayed.

"Just totally lucky," Washburn said. "I didn't even have a bed for a long time. I just had a sleeping bag, and I would roll it out and sleep in the living room. The place was wall-to-wall carpet with no furniture, and I'd just lay there and look out the window in the morning and check the surf. And that was a fantasy world to me."

Aside from the astronomical rent, Washburn had it dialed. He could surf early or late; sometimes the midafternoon was wide open. Ocean Beach was a vast expanse of usable spots, meaning no one place ever got too crowded. And the scale of what awaited Washburn each day awed him. Compared with the Jersey shore, the 25-foot faces that often rose up at O.B. were epic, and the sandbar across the street from his apartment carried the best waves he'd ever seen, perfect big barrels. If you got pounded, you simply got washed onto the beach.

It took Doc Renneker to get Washburn down to Maverick's for his first visit in 1992, just two years after Jeff Clark corralled Dave Schmidt and Tom Powers from the parking lot at O.B. Renneker, a respected practitioner of alternative medicine in the city and legendary surfer up and down the coast, had already trekked to Pillar Point enough times to want to share the place with others; but Washburn could initially think of no good reason why he would want to go. He loved the idea and the image of the huge waves at Maverick's, but he wasn't sure he liked the notion of actually attempting them. He had a happy thing going right outside his front door. And when money was tight, which it always was, what was the point of surfing in a place where, if you got caught inside the wave, your precious board was quite likely to be smashed into pieces?

But Renneker persisted, and, as often happened with Doc, he finally prevailed. After having surfed several times with Washburn at Ocean Beach and realizing that the two were actually neighbors who lived on the same block, Renneker got Grant into a car and took the ride down the coast to Princeton and the harbor. Washburn made the twenty-minute walk from the gravel parking lot out to the point, looked on the wave breaking a half mile beyond, and realized pretty quickly that his life had changed.

Over the next decade and a half, by Bruce Jenkins's estimate, no person surfed Maverick's more often than Grant Washburn. Even as his life went through its inevitable permutations, his big-gun board was seldom dry for long. Washburn left construction and began moving toward a career as a videographer and documentarian. He married. He became a father twice over. But he surfed off Pillar Point before, during, and after all of that time. Essentially, Washburn grew into adulthood while riding the massive faces of Mavs.

Washburn's constant presence in the lineup led him to a

deep and thorough knowledge of the wave in all of its different incarnations, and as his understanding of the force grew, he became more and more determined to surf it at every possible opportunity. He understood it well enough to recognize that he would not be able to ride Maverick's indefinitely. It was not that kind of experience; it was temporal. And it mattered. To Grant, the wave came to symbolize everything he really knew about life. It was all there in the water, in that massive force. It was a thing that, like life, could be only partially understood. It certainly could change without warning. A winter at Maverick's was often days and days of smooth, glassy tedium, followed by a few hours of the most intense, blood-rushing activity attempted anywhere on the planet. It felt like the wrath of God when it came, and you were either in or you were out. This wasn't a halfway kind of a venture. Every scrap of knowledge gleaned was invaluable.

"It's the only thing I was ever interested in surfing—the big waves," Washburn said. "I do think when people are born, they either have a fascination with something like this or they don't. Even a guy who is a great surfer and a great athlete can't be made to do this. Part of him might want to, the sponsors might want him to, there might be a lot of reasons why he should be able to do it; but if he doesn't really like it, he's gonna be miserable. And there is going to be some other guy who might have no talent at all, who has a total fascination with it. And that passion and the drive will get him there."

Washburn knew riders who were inelegant on their boards yet still able to catch the giant waves at Maverick's, because they were fit and confident and wanted that challenge. It was a remarkably low percentage of the available surfers, though. "There are tens of thousands of people who would paddle out to Maverick's, but there are only a few hundred—if that— who would really ride the wave on a big day," he said. "And we all know that none of us is going to kick its ass. It will, if it gets us, kill any one of us on a whim. But when you're feeling it, you don't think about any of that. You're just in the zone, like when you're playing basketball and you can't miss a shot. There is no fear, no lump in your throat. You just can't wait for the next wave, because you're so sure you are going to get it. Those moments are few and far between, but they keep you going, because in that moment you are not fighting it at all. You're using its own energy. It all becomes very clear out there."

Washburn pursued knowledge of the wave like a hungry student; he couldn't get enough. He surfed on glorious days and flat, uninviting days. He learned what kind of risk was acceptable in the giant barrels. He figured out how to surf the nastiest wave in North America without getting himself blown up or even seriously wiping out. Along the way, he became one of the leading voices on the wave and one of the de facto leaders of the hardcore big-wave surfing element in Northern California. His fascination with Maverick's led him into a strong friendship with Jeff Clark, and as he slowly became able to afford grander, more precise surfboards, he ordered most of them from Clark.

The two men developed a relationship based on mutual respect and a love of the wave itself. And they shared a desire to know everything that there was to know about Mavs, a desire that passed mere surf enthusiasm and eventually moved them, however warily, into the realms of science. Over time, it moved both men into the area of Mark Sponsler's specialty.

IN THE LOFT OF a two-story house just off Five Canyons Parkway, about an hour's drive from the coast, perched on a hill where the homes of the Castro Valley at night spread out like a lighted floor beneath him, Mark Sponsler studies his computer models and thinks. He is trying to simply explain the scientific phenomena that eventually result in 50- or 75-foot waves dropping in at Maverick's. The story begins with wind—and, sometimes, too, it can end there.

"The thing that makes surf is wind," Sponsler is saying. Set about him like little sphinxes, five computers whir lightly in the background. Four monitors, positioned at various intervals around the L-shaped wooden desk that sinks down into the padded carpet, display a constantly rotating series of readings, charts, and graphs. Halfway across the country, in Chicago, two web servers are pressed into duty. Three of Sponsler's computer towers run twenty-four hours a day, building the wave models and weather forecasts that ultimately inform his declarations about what it is going to look like the next time Greg Long or Jeff Clark put into the water at Maverick's—or anywhere else around the West Coast, for that matter.

Over the past several years, Sponsler's web site, Stormsurf .com, has become a destination for anyone who is serious about surfing Mavs more than once or twice per winter. With its detailed analysis and a swell-potential forecast that breaks down the calculations into an easy-to-follow one-to-ten scale, with ten indicating massive, can't-believe-your-eyes waves, Stormsurf.com is routinely a part of any conversation about Maverick's and its conditions. It doesn't hurt that Sponsler likes to ride the waves there too, nor that he has become a regular face in the lineup. "I'm forecasting the surf so that I know when I want to go surfing," he says with an easy laugh.

The entire natural spectacle of Maverick's is rooted in the storms that form off the coast of Japan, out over the open water, where low pressure moving up from Siberia collides with the warmer air currents coming off the island. The resulting forces kick-start the action and create the winds. The winds, Sponsler says, generate friction as they blow across the surface of the water, literally moving or dragging the water in the process and creating wave-trains of energy that begin making their way across thousands of miles of ocean. The ultimate size of the swells depends upon on how fast the wind is blowing, the area over which the wind blows (the "fetch," or the size of the storm), and the duration of the storm. Eventually, the journey will end on the shores of California.

That intricate dance still amazes Sponsler, who by now has studied it for years. Though he might not evince much wetsuit admiration while locked in behind his bank of computer monitors, close-focusing on complicated formulas and distant wind and weather readings, Sponsler is consulted on a round-the-clock basis anytime there is a chance that a swell might reach Half Moon Bay under conditions that would favor a contest. That is, anytime the energy waves somehow make their way entirely across the North Pacific without running out of steam, spreading out too wide, or getting sheared off somewhere like the Farallons, a group of islands and sea-stacks some 27 miles west of the Golden Gate and the coast of San Francisco. The storms have to move at a precise angle, carry sufficient speed, and not have anything get in their way in order to ultimately arrive at Maverick's. It is the meteorological equivalent of fitting a camel through the eye of a needle.

And that's just to get reasonable waves to the surf point on any old day. For the contest itself, Sponsler says, "The criterion, ideally, is 20-foot Hawaiian, with no winds, from 290 to 295 degrees (on the compass, meaning the wave is approaching from a westerly direction that will allow it to shoal and break at Maverick's) with the tide, a two-foot tide preferably, and holding that in a four-hour window to get from the first heat through to the finals. On a Monday through a Friday. In the daylight hours. Oh, and it all has to occur during the contest window, whether that opens in November or January."

Sponsler chuckles. "It's like hitting the sweet spot on a golf club. You can literally draw a little box on a map and say, 'If the storm doesn't go through this tiny space at exactly the right angle and with the right speed at the right time, then forget it. It'll never get here.' If it manages to go through that exact right area, then I'll say, 'Okay, now I'm interested.'"

It sounds miraculous, and yet over the course of a normal winter at Half Moon Bay, those conditions will in fact prevail a great number of times. The critical component of the conversation usually happens *after* the storm finally arrives at Maverick's.

Sponsler rattles off a list of the things that, for the surfers, can compromise a great swell even after it has traversed the open ocean and is bearing down on Mavs. "You can get 20-footers right as the sun is setting, and then by the time morning rolls back around, the action is already fading and gone. Or it comes and goes and you've got a six-foot tide in the middle of the day (thus diminishing the wave), and you're screwed. Or it comes, but a cold front comes with it and the wind is blowing out of the south, and you can't do it. Any of a billion things."

The most difficult factor is probably the wind—local wind in particular. Just about everything else about the surf point and the swells will be rendered inconsequential if the wind blows too hard in one direction or another, but especially from the south—the offshore breeze that goes out to sea directly toward the surf point, and thus stands up the waves or even knocks them slightly backward as they break. "If there's any wind at all, if it's an offshore wind, that's heinous. You can't even drop down the face—it just blows you out the back of the wave," Sponsler says. "If the wind is out of the south, then there's a stair-step chop running up the face of the wave, and it's like trying to surf on a mogul field. You just don't do that. It's stupid."

The waves that reach Maverick's, be they inconsequential sprays or thick, towering masses, are all liquid pulses of energy. Toby Garfield, a physical oceanographer at San Francisco State University, calls the process of delivering that energy all the way across the Pacific a "harmonic motion," as opposed to the cresting wave many would imagine at sea. Says Garfield, "It's just like you had a spring with a weight on it, and you pull it down and let it go, and you just watch it undulate. When I say 'wave,' I'm thinking of the whole series of how that energy moves. Not just one wave—it's a series of waves." Drop a penny into a bucket of water and you see energy pulsing toward the sides. Drop a rock into that same bucket and you'll begin to approximate Maverick's-sized wave energy.

Still, the uniqueness of Maverick's lies in how the point concentrates and transfers that energy. Some 21 feet below the ocean's surface, half a mile out to sea, the outer reef has been shaped and honed over millions of years, dating to the layers of sedimentary rock that began forming during the Pliocene (5.3 million to 1.6 million years ago) and were further built over time by sand sediment that anchored to the top of the rock. Over the centuries, less resistant rock beds around it deteriorated and eroded into troughs. But the Maverick's reef formed and continued to build as an upward-sloping structure, very much like a ski jump.

The reef is also narrower than most of the waves that approach it, which explains nearly everything about the size of the ensuing throws. As Toby Garfield often tells aspiring students of Maverick's, the energy within a wave is ultimately conserved—that is, it remains constant. The energy may vary back and forth between the wave's speed and its height, but it always adds up to the same amount. Thus, if a wave slows down, it automatically gains in height in order to preserve all of its energy. And as it approaches the underwater reef at Maverick's, its energy becomes concentrated in the smaller space of the ramp. The wave slows, but it builds height to compensate. The sheer force, the energy the wave has carried across the open ocean, ultimately determines the height once it reaches the upper levels of the rising reef.

In 2007, the National Oceanic and Atmospheric Administration (NOAA) completed an ambitious survey that demonstrated in graphic detail the forces that combine to make Maverick's the beast it is. Working with the California Ocean Protection Council, NOAA staffers bounced sound and light off the ocean floor in a series of overlapping images, thus producing a three-dimensional look at the entire central California coast seafloor. The maps revealed details that surprised even veteran researchers. First, the reef-ramp at Maverick's is significantly taller and more built-up than anyone had suspected. Second, the ocean beds on either side of the reef, worn down over the eons, play host to exceptionally calm and deep water, which allow the approaching waves to draw even more energy as they blast up the ramp. It is the most extraordinary combination of circumstances. As one expert put it, "I've done an awful lot of seafloor mapping, and I've never seen geology like that before."

"The shape of the reef focuses that wave into a point right there," Garfield says. "So if you're talking to Grant Washburn or someone who surfs it, they'll say, 'You're just sitting here and those waves pop up.' Well, you're taking the energy that was spread over a pretty wide distance and you're focusing it over a pretty small distance. It's like a kid with a magnifying glass—the lens on the glass takes light over a bigger area and focuses it in a smaller area. The shape of the bottom, the reef, acts like a magnifying glass for the waves that are coming in."

The wave heights that result can move from impressive

to astonishing to unrideable over the course of an hour. Maverick's is generally known for 40- and 50-foot wave faces, but only because those are the upper limits of what has been considered safe to ride—and certainly to paddle into. They don't represent the true ceiling by any means.

In the 1990s, Laird Hamilton and a host of colleagues began to redefine what was possible on a surfboard, combining their love of the waves with the power of modern machinery. The advent of tow-in surfing, championed by Hamilton and other hard-chargers in Hawaii, changed the landscape of surfing forever. The surfers used ropes attached to Jet Skis or helicopters to get themselves towed into giant waves from the side, rather than having to paddle to the top, surf down the face and risk catastrophic falls. The process allowed Hamilton and others to traverse waves that would have been impossible to catch otherwise.

Tow surfers have since gone on to chase and challenge the largest waves on the planet, tracking down 100-footers with the help of private watercraft, or PWC. At Maverick's, which sits in a small corner of the Monterey Bay National Marine Sanctuary, the practice is profoundly controversial, with equally passionate people on both sides debating the environmental impact of using engine-driven (and thus polluting) craft in the surf area. It's clear, however, that any surfer using a PWC to tow him is going to be able to catch waves that would close out a paddle surfer on sheer height alone. For his love of the pure joy of taking on a wave himself and his certainty that the safety of the surfers may depend on it, Jeff Clark is still among those willing to use PWCs to catch waves on days when paddling is out of the question—and Clark is foursquare behind the idea of using the Jet Skis for rescue missions of all kinds.

Even then, though, Maverick's during the winter routinely produces conditions—huge waves, treacherous churning water, sudden breaks toward the jagged inner reef—that preclude surfers under any circumstances from going out and trying, unless it is a death wish they're pursuing. Watercraft or no, the point becomes a hostile force. That is its raw, physical nature. For all of its attraction to champion big-wave riders and the cadre of other hardy souls who annually make the pilgrimage to Half Moon Bay, Maverick's at its most fierce is capable of scaring off virtually everyone.

One such day occurred in 2001, when an afternoon set of waves began to escalate in size and strength exponentially, first chasing away the paddle surfers and then, as the heights reached well beyond 60 feet and toward 80 feet and gained in thickness and ferocity, the tow-in crew as well. In the end, only two people remained on the water: Shawn Alladio and J. C. Cahill, a pair of safety patrollers on their Jet Skis who had come for the day as rescue crew for the surfers. As the two worked the water, seeing everyone safely out, they looked to the horizon; a huge set was thundering toward them. It was unlike anything either of them had ever seen at Maverick's, bigger and faster, bearing down at incredible speed. They soon realized that they had no chance of getting to the shoulder of the wave before it crashed down on top of them and sent them hurtling toward the inner reef.

Adrenaline kicked in, a survival instinct. Alladio, the

more experienced of the two drivers, determined that their only chance was to gun their engines and sprint directly toward the swells—to meet them head-on and try to get over them before they crested and slammed down in full big-wave fury. Miraculously, they succeeded, going up and over each of the half-dozen ensuing faces, traversing the gaping troughs of water, waves so huge that the afternoon was subsequently to be dubbed One Hundred Foot Wednesday. Scurrying back to the safe harbor after the set rolled through, Alladio knew she and Cahill had been extraordinarily lucky. She also took in a set of sensory experiences that she would not forget.

"Normally," Alladio later told the *San Francisco Chronicle*, "when you go over a big wave, you get pelted with the spray, like raindrops, on the other side. But these clots of water were huge, the size of your fist, and they exploded like you were getting pounded by water balloons. And on the wave fronts, each time we went up I could see all these fissures or ravines in the surface, and there was some kind of crazy light energy vibrating inside the wave like electricity. And I remember thinking, 'Those are the fingers of God.'"

When it isn't brutalizing people, Maverick's often inspires such thoughts. It is a force so immense that few comparisons are apt. Mark Sponsler grew up in Cocoa Beach, Florida, surfing in gentle, waist-high foam just about every day. He was part of a regular surfing crew, several years older than one of the other locals there, a boy whose surfing prowess was evident from an early age: Kelly Slater. When Sponsler moved to Northern California with his wife in 1994, he was totally unprepared for the height, thickness, and ferocity of the waves that broke off the Pacific; it was a genuinely moving sight. "It was like going from sandlot baseball to the major leagues overnight," he says. "Being from Florida, I had been to Hawaii a bunch of times, because that was the big-wave mecca. And Hawaii has got great surf. But Maverick's is a step up—a whole order of magnitude. It's thicker, it breaks much harder, it's a longer wave, and it breaks small and it breaks huge. You surf in Hawaii and you think you know what you're doing on a big wave, but you have no clue about Maverick's."

Realizing that he had to start over as a big-wave surfer, Sponsler sought out Jeff Clark in Princeton by the Sea to build him a board that was made for the kind of riding he wanted to do at Maverick's. From that first transaction, a relationship was born; and when Sponsler later began to dabble in wave and weather forecasting, he shared his early results with Jeff, who was already basically doing the same thing, with cruder instrumentation, from the apartment he was then renting.

Jeff wanted to incorporate Mark's thoughts and ideas, and eventually Sponsler started writing them down in e-mails that the two shot back and forth between the coast and Castro Valley. Other surfers got word and asked to be included in the e-mail chain. Now, years later, Sponsler had a thriving web site that took most of his free time when he wasn't working his job developing software systems for the Kaiser Permanente medical giant, and he found himself trying to help the surfers figure out whether to call the contest that his friend Jeff always used to run. But that didn't mean that Clark was out of the picture. That would be impossible. Jeff Clark was still front and center in almost everything related to Maverick's.

Jeff's presence in the current mess was one more reminder to Grant Washburn that things had changed radically from those first few heady years that he surfed the point, content simply to be on the water and try to figure things out. Washburn's experience now was complicated by his knowledge of all things connected with Mavs, not just the wave. He had been granted a firsthand look at the evolving nature of the sport and of the industry.

Among other things, Grant saw Flea Virostko grow from a young hellion into a national and international sponsorship sensation, a guy whose outlandish lifestyle and willingness to take absurd, even stupid risks wound up paying him more than he could have made doing almost anything else he was remotely qualified to do. It was, for Washburn, a revelation about the nature of the business that orbited his and his friends' habit of trying to climb mountains made of water.

The dynamic of recklessness was fairly common among the surfers. After all, several of them had been paid greater or smaller sums over the years to portray themselves as guys who didn't care about what the rest of the world wanted because they were too busy being stoked out of their minds by the waves and the great party scene all around them. Before and during his now-public alcohol and crystal meth addictions, Flea found that being a bad boy could have amazing rewards. At one point, he was pulling in upward of $150,000 a year from various endorsements and sponsorships that were predicated on two things: his willingness to attack just about any wave anywhere, and his eagerness to live up to his reputation as a partying wild man who was ripping his way through life.

Flea jumped in with abandon, which was mostly fine with everyone. Bad behavior was essentially rewarded. For Virostko to miss an interview with a local TV crew because he was too hung over, had hit the surf early, or had just plain overslept was, in a very direct way, exactly what the image of him called for. What frustrated some people in the short term was actually thought of as effective branding for the companies in the long term.

"It was like they were rewarding him for being kind of a derelict," a friend said. "Flea was pulling in 10k, 12k a month, and that's pretty good money for doing nothing, hanging around. If he blew off stuff and didn't show up, that's cool—it makes him more of an institution, a surf punk, and that's what the companies were selling." In the water, the effect of the stimulants in particular on Flea's system was undeniable: he could be an absolute beast on the waves of Maverick's, out of all proportion to the toll that his percentage of failed rides should have been taking on his body. "His stamina, his endurance—everything was sharper," another surfer said. "He would take these horrible wipeouts and just pop right back up. It wasn't human."

It was chemical, and the true depths of Flea's addictions were not known to most of the big-wave world until the spring of 2009, when *Surfer* magazine writer and editor Kimball Taylor produced a compelling, multilayered view of Virostko as a user. Written with Flea's full cooperation as the surfer moved through a recovery regimen, the story laid bare his vices and regrets and explained the meth craze that had ripped through Santa Cruz and up and down the Northern

Coast. Included was the grim reality that Flea's drug habit had caused him to burn through all the money those sponsorships had ever paid him and that he was, at the time of Kimball's writing, living little better than hand-to-mouth, with most of his things repossessed or sold off to pay back taxes and other debts. Perhaps most startling of all was Flea's acknowledgment that he was high on acid the very first time he surfed Maverick's, as a twenty-year-old in the early 1990s, and that he had surfed the wave scores of times while high. On his way to Pacific Grove to check in to rehab in 2008, Flea said he chugged a bottle of vodka and smoked a pipe of crystal. He introduced himself to the facility by blowing a .28 on the blood-alcohol meter.

"I went to the edge of the earth," he said.

His surfing peers were almost as shocked to discover, in the same *Surfer* magazine article, fellow Santa Cruz west-sider Peter Mel's admission that he, too, had become addicted to crystal meth for a time before finally getting sober. Mel was one of the pillars of the Maverick's community, perhaps the most trusted voice on the waves. Both he and Flea represented the best of Santa Cruz surfing—fearless, inventive, athletic— but Pete also was regarded as something of a caretaker of Maverick's, a kind of unofficial guardian of the soul of the place. His willingness to speak frankly to the magazine on the meth topic, despite his deep personal embarrassment at having fallen into using the drug before pulling himself out of trouble and into a twelve-step program, was a wake-up call for some. For many of the surfers, drug use was a familiar but seldom-discussed subject—"Doing drugs was just fun and acceptable among my friends," Flea said—and it was of limited interest once everyone was on the water. But when big-wave favorite Peter Davi died in December 2007 while surfing at Ghost Tree, a break near Monterey, and when the coroner's report listed "acute methamphetamine intoxication" as a potential contributing factor, tongues began to loosen. Flea's article sparked a full-fledged conversation.

"Very strange," said Bruce Jenkins, the *San Francisco Chronicle* columnist. "With the crystal meth, I didn't even know. It doesn't even really make sense. Surfing giant waves has a flow to it. It's not a fast-twitch kind of reaction. It is very measured, and you get into the wave and you make your turn, and if you fall you just kind of react."

Flea's public acknowledgment, however necessary, was a wrenching moment for Jeff Clark. As much as Clark understood the forces that might drive friends to substance use, it pained him to see his friends publicly identified as addicts, even as recovering addicts. He felt the weight of Maverick's there. People should be talking about the amazing waves, but instead they were talking about Flea and Pete Mel and the drug scene on the Highway 1 corridor during the early nineties. Jeff knew as well as anyone how difficult it was to capture the high Maverick's provided anywhere else, and he thought he understood that, in trying to get there, some people might wind up turning to drugs as a dry-land alternative. But he felt protective of the group of surfers who had the stones to ride the wave and the spirit to really connect with the place. It wasn't unusual at Maverick's to find utterly disparate souls like Flea and Doc Renneker, that erudite, sometimes abrasive member of the old guard, hanging out, laughing and talking together. The wave, and respect for it, superseded practically all of the factors that would prevent some of the surfers from ever speaking to one another out of the water. Jeff would never sell out anyone in the water. It was how he processed things. He didn't judge his friends. And for that reason, among many others, Jeff's circle of friends seemed to grow ever wider.

Drugs aside, Flea's commercial success was, to Washburn, more akin to modeling than to sport. Grant was able to separate Flea the surfer from Flea the marketing opportunity. On the water, Washburn and Flea got along famously, and Grant often noted that of all the rough-and-tumble Santa Cruz surfers who could make life miserable for an outsider, Flea was consistently the person who found a kind word for someone in an unexpected or difficult moment. On a flight to South Africa to begin a surfing expedition, Grant observed Virostko help passenger after passenger get their luggage situated overhead so they could sit more comfortably, and then watched as Flea reacted to the poverty he encountered on the ground by handing out money to almost every person he passed who appeared to be in need. Flea was a deeply human young guy who happened to be getting paid to act like he didn't give a rat's ass about anybody, and the drinking and drug use that often brought out the beast in him, while real, was also part of the very thing that sponsors found so attractive.

"He was iconic, and he was also gregarious and just a big, outgoing personality, and that's what they were all kind of taking from him," Washburn said. "It did make him the life of the party wherever he went. I had other friends who were the life of the party, and none of them can drink anymore. And part of that character trait is, they're just not going to go home. If you don't make them go home, they'll keep going until tomorrow night. They're the 10 percent of the population like that, and they need some place to put all that energy or they'll keep chasing a high. For Michael Phelps, swimming was it. They're going to put him on ADD medication, he's probably going to wind up the fat kid in the back of the class—and instead, he's got all these medals, greatest swimmer ever, all that. Flea's like that, and he got paid. I always told Greg Long, who didn't get a deal for two years after he was clearly established as the dominant guy, that he should shave his head and get a tattoo on his face. He'd have had a deal within a week."

By dint of his early association with the break, Washburn got a firsthand look at the growing industry around it, which took in the likes of Flea. He also was a witness to the growing international popularity of the wave itself, for better and for worse.

Grant had been surfing the point for two years when Mark Foo and Ken Bradshaw arrived from Hawaii in December 1994 to try the epic swell that itself had just arrived. Washburn had delayed a trip to his parents' home in Florida so that he could stay an extra day or two and surf some more. He understood all about the allure of the wave.

The fact that Foo died, on December 23, 1994, on a day described as "ordinary" by several people was not lost on Washburn, because he knew that the conditions that week had been anything but ordinary. "Ordinary," in the language of those who didn't actually surf the wave, simply meant that the height as measured on the face or the back didn't clear some historic bar; but Maverick's that day was treacherous, with twenty-second intervals between waves, fast-moving walls of water and sets that produced multiple breakers. Several riders took epic spills—it was that week that Jay Moriarity's gigantic wipeout (dubbed "The Crucifixion") produced photos that splashed on magazine covers worldwide. Most who wiped out were fortunate to survive with relatively minor injuries. Foo, who had flown overnight with Bradshaw just to reach the point in time to surf, took what appeared to be a routine fall. Just two years into his tenure, Grant Washburn knew that there was no such thing as a routine fall at Maverick's.

Part of the allure of the wave, even before Mark Foo's death, was the sense of looming danger for all who dared to ride it. The thrill was inescapable. Most of the riders had no death wish, but every one of them felt connected with and even addicted to the rush of adrenaline that accompanied taking the risk. Maverick's was, in essence, this very cool thing to do that could also kill you if you did it wrong. Long before Foo arrived from Hawaii, the Nor Cal big-wave crew knew all about that, and they took it seriously.

No one has ever suggested that Mark Foo did not. Matt Warshaw's book, with its extensive recounting of December 23, 1994, never intimates otherwise. It's true that Foo was one of surfing's most outlandish showmen, and it is equally true that Foo never went anywhere to surf without alerting photographers to where he would be; but there is nothing in the video and photo documents of his final ride to suggest that he was taking an outrageous chance or was even positioned poorly on the wave. The idea that Foo mostly was doing things right, in fact, is the most chilling aspect of his death to those who continue to surf Maverick's.

In the weeks after Foo's death, Grant Washburn studied the evidence for hours at a time, trying to piece together an answer that might lessen the dread he felt in his heart. His ultimate conclusion was of little comfort. Mark Foo died, Grant decided, because he was unlucky. That was it. "But that's what you're messing with," Washburn said. "He went right down the wave in the spot where, in Hawaii, he would've gotten away with it. But Maverick's has this little wedge, and you see a lot of guys crashing onto it forward, like they're going over the handlebars of a bike. It's almost invisible. It's not obvious that it's going to happen, and it owes to the shape of the reef itself. When the wave hits the first part of the reef, it's kind of a normal wave, and then it hits the next part, which is an underwater bulkhead, and when it hits that thing, it shifts. And if you fall right there, you're in the middle of it."

Foo lost control of his board on the inside rail and smacked suddenly into the mid-face of the wave. The barrel sucked him up in its giant roll and threw him back over the falls as it slammed deep into the impact zone. A surfer on the next wave in the set, Mike Parsons, was similarly dumped into the zone, and as he hurtled underwater toward the Boneyard, Parsons is believed to have unknowingly bumped into Foo, who may or may not have been conscious at that time. Parsons was violently flushed into the rocks, but he survived his ordeal. Foo never surfaced, although in all the activity and raucousness of the wave and the lineup that day, his absence wasn't immediately noticed. Everyone knew that Foo had taken a severe wipeout, but on the surface it did not look markedly worse than what anyone else had absorbed. Practically anyone who fell was in for a multiple-wave hold-down, given the brief interval between waves and the speed of the barrels. Most of the riders assumed Foo had broken his board and gone in to get another one or to retire for the day. They were universally stunned to learn that he hadn't made it.

Washburn knew more. He had surfed the point so many times, in so many conditions, and taken wipeouts from so many angles that he knew it was not unusual for surfers to sustain a concussion from falling in the spot where Foo went down. Even if you didn't black out, the explosive force of being sucked into the falls and thrown over could be disorienting to the point of helplessness underwater. He'd been there, as had most of the others. It was practically an occupational hazard. But it also carried with it the threat of something irreversible going wrong, which was one reason that Washburn, with each passing year, had become more and more selective about the waves he'd ride. He wasn't going over the falls. He wasn't going deep into the pit, down into the trench. Terrible things could happen there.

There were no physical signs of major trauma to Mark Foo's body, nor was there evidence of a concussion. Doc Renneker, after examining the body, speculated that Foo probably got caught on the bottom of the deep trench, his leash hung up on a stony projection or something jutting up off the ocean floor. Washburn's first theory was simple: Foo drowned. Either he got knocked out by the sheer force of his initial fall or he blacked out during the extended hold-down of the ensuing waves, but drowning was the most likely and most supportable conclusion. It was devastating; it was stunning; but it also was, in Washburn's view, just plain bad luck. And that was the knowledge that Washburn carried with him. As the years passed and the risks that the surfers were willing to assume inexorably grew, it was a knowledge he hoped to share.

"The thing to remember, for these guys, is that now we're riding it when it's much bigger than that—way heavier," he said. "Guys maybe don't want to know, some of them, or to listen about it—like Twiggy. I'm always trying to say to him to be careful. They need that mentality that says they can go for it, but at the same time, you'd rather have them grow old. I've always said that. This wave can get *way* heavier than what people can handle. I don't care how many laps you did in your pool, how many rounds you did in the boxing ring, your Brazilian training, your jujitsu, your running with the rock—it's not going to matter after this wave gets to a certain point on any given day. Mavs is different. Just getting out of the water in one piece is a good thing."

Washburn's eloquence about the wave, his filmmaker's eye for detail, and his constant presence and good cheer in the lineup combined to elevate him to a position of prominence among the Maverick's regulars. Along with Pete Mel, Washburn was considered a go-to source for surfers and the media alike. Jeff trusted him, and once Keir began to understand the concept of the contest itself, he quickly added Washburn to his small circle of automatic calls. Keir brought in Grant to help with some of the shows that MSV would try to farm out to places like Fuel TV. He included him in many of the conversations about the status of the contest: what it took to make a swell contestable, what the weather conditions in general needed to be, the logistical process of putting everything in place on the day of the event. Grant had been on board for every Mavs contest ever run, and even if he was personally ambivalent about the idea of such a thing, he wasn't going to stand in the way. He didn't really care if MSV or Keir figured out a way to squeeze profit out of it. If it was good for the surfers and good for the place, he was in. In the largest moments, Grant Washburn tended to keep things simple. What he didn't know at the time was that he was accumulating the experience he would need to someday assume the leadership role entirely.

Chapter 9

J EFF CLARK AND CHRIS BERTISH made their way up Highway 1 in Jeff's SUV, snaking toward the El Granada condo that Clark now shared with his third wife, Cassandra. On their drive in from the SFO airport, Chris Bertish had thought things through and realized that he had what he needed. Brutal trip aside, missing equipment aside, he had it. He had Jeff Clark, surfboard shaper supreme, on his side. And Jeff had in his possession a nine-foot two-inch Jeff Clark Original, which just happened to be Chris Bertish's favorite backup board. They finally reached Half Moon Bay at about 1 a.m. It was by then officially the day of the February 13, 2010 Maverick's Big Wave Contest, and the morning sky would begin to lighten sooner than either man could imagine.

When they got to the condo, Jeff jumped into action; he wasn't going to rest until he got Chris set up. They carefully worked over the board, making sure the fins were set to Chris's specifications and that come morning he could roll out to the competition with everything ready to go. Despite the late hour, Jeff worked with the efficiency and enthusiasm of a guy half his age. With the prospect of a great day in the water on the horizon, it was as if Jeff himself were the one headed for the contest. If anyone needed to understand why so many of the surfers had stood by Jeff over the years, this was the most basic of examples. In the toughest moments, Jeff often shone.

The months since Jeff's ouster as contest director had been tumultuous. First, the twenty-four invited surfers themselves had to work on the mechanical means to arrive at a group consensus on whether to green-light the event. As Keir had promised, the window of opportunity opened on November 1, and the surfers eventually found that the most efficient thing to do was simply to text or e-mail—cell phone to cell phone—most of their conversation about possible days to surf. But their communication was uneven at best, and fate intervened in the early days in the wickedest fashion. There were absolutely surfable sessions—in fact, the tremendous swells and sets were piling up one upon the other—but the backdrop for so many of the days was overcast or dark, brooding skies. For the surfers, the photographers, and the videographers, what made a contest day into an iconic moment were the truly classic conditions: wave faces of 40 feet or taller set against a high blue sky and brilliant sun. Those conditions meant posters that sold and the photos that made magazine covers. Those waves, ridden expertly in such eye-popping colors, earned global awards and possibly even some modest financial payouts.

On top of that, several of the very best days ran into mundane scheduling issues that had derailed many a potential contest effort in years past. One of the best swells of the season arrived on Thanksgiving Day—not the weekend, but the day itself. The Christmas period was largely blacked out as a contest consideration, yet the waves around that time were virtually perfect, with nice atmospherics to boot. November yielded to December and then to January, the early window essentially squandered. A couple of proposed votes went down in flames when Mark Sponsler informed the crew that offshore winds likely would turn their beloved wave to mush or make conditions too harsh. Several of the top surfers began to worry that the best chance for an epic Maverick's 2009 contest had already passed. Some could count five or six missed dates already. The guys were finding out that calling the event was no simple feat.

At the same time, the surfers' collective relationship with Jeff was still sorting itself out. In the immediate aftermath of his firing, several of the guys openly pondered whether it was disloyal to even consider participating in the Maverick's Surf Contest. "He's still the man out there, and he has been a friend to all of us over the years," Pete Mel noted. But it didn't take long for Mel and Washburn and Greg Long and the others to conclude that the contest itself was special and important—and that they wouldn't be sacrificing their friendship with Clark by participating in it.

"We all realized how important this event is to us," Mel

said. "It's one of the great surf contests in the world. We agreed that we had to keep it going, whether Jeff was in it or not. And I think he understands that."

It was the result that Keir Beadling had been counting on, but Beadling might have been surprised to learn that Clark had made a personal decision to lay low when it came to his surfing buddies. Jeff applied no pressure on the subject of the contest. Whether or not he understood what any of his friends were doing, he wasn't going to stand in the way of their gathering on a great day with the chance to record incredible rides and collect the kinds of paychecks that most of them would rarely see as surfers. Jeff spent most of the summer of '09 rehabbing his hip and considering his options. As much as he had wanted to be rid of Keir and MSV, the actual endgame had brought him little peace. Having his own event taken away from him was not the outcome Jeff had imagined when he thought of divorcing himself from the corporate types who were trying to invade his little corner of the sport. He lived with the notion that he had brought the trouble on himself by reaching out and striking a deal with Keir in the first place. It was on Jeff that it had happened at all, even if he could honestly plead that he hadn't really known where it would lead.

When it came to Maverick's, Jeff was possessed of the kind of intuition and feel about the place that could be difficult to explain. Bruce Jenkins once marveled at how many times Clark's premonition about the conditions on a given day at the point turned out to be virtually 100 percent on target, and Washburn reminded him that there were at least two memorable contest days—Twiggy's surprise win in 2006 and Greg Long's great rides of 2008—that never would have been run if anyone but Jeff had been making the call. And yet Jeff had helped lead to this intensely awkward moment in their surfing lives. In the end, it was a case of the less said, the better. The only move that made any sense was the one that took the surfers toward the water.

The media came and went, with a big flurry of stories about Jeff getting pushed out followed by weeks of silence. Since no one knew exactly where the apparently rudderless contest was headed, the mainstream press looked the other way and the surfing media pondered the situation without any notion of a resolution. Keir went back to work trying to expand the Maverick's brand, and an abbreviated Maverick's Concert Tour was planned. Executives at Barracuda, though perhaps confused by the fact that Beadling had accepted their sponsorship just before he severed ties with the only person ever famously associated with Maverick's, decided to stay in for the 2009–10 season. Keir had his funding and his November 1 contest window opening.

By late summer, Clark was back in the water, able to navigate around by standing up on a board and using a long paddle to take him where he wanted to go. His SUP, or stand-up paddle board, was actually an ancient Hawaiian form of surfing that was beginning to gain popularity among riders because it allowed them to see the incoming sets much more clearly; but all Jeff cared about was that he could get back to the ocean this way. His friends noticed a marked difference in his mood. Jeff was diligent in his rehab work and was beginning to recover flexibility in his hip; he was having fun again. And his ability to get on an SUP provided Jeff another opportunity: to greet his friends on a mutually acceptable spot on the earth.

It was late October when that finally happened to a memorable end, at the opening ceremony for the 2009–10 big-wave contest. Over the years, the ceremony had come to stand as an important and spiritual part of the whole deal. The surfers met on the beach at Pillar Point, posed for a few photos, heard a couple of welcoming speeches, and then had the opportunity to say a few words themselves. On this day, under a cool, low sky, Pete Mel stepped forward to explain to the assembled crowd what would happen next: the surfers would paddle out a short way into the water, to a place where they were the only ones who could hear what was said. They would form a circle in the water, holding hands and saying prayers for a good season, safe journeys, and epic rides. If someone wanted to speak, he was met with approval and support. "Each and every time we go out, we get together to honor this very special spot," Pete said. "And we honor some of our fallen comrades and remember them—especially guys like Jay Moriarity, who should be sitting right here in this lineup, Peter Davi, Mark Foo—and we go out there as surfers. That's what we do. We unite. But as we move into this new chapter of the event, all of these guys are going to have a big role in what we do going forward."

Greg Long spoke of the honor he felt at being able to surf Maverick's. Flea Virostko, newly sober and in the process of opening his own program, Fleahab, that was designed to teach addicts to surf, mentioned his memories of first approaching the big wave as a twenty-year-old and thinking to himself, "This is going to be a brutal twenty years. I'm going to get beat up out here." He did not realize at the time how many of his wounds over the next decade and a half would be self-inflicted. "Watch out for other people," Flea said with a wink. The crowd, understanding exactly what he meant, burst into applause.

The photographers moved in for the annual shot of the men lined up in a row along the beach, their huge boards propped skyward behind them. The men then began the short paddle-out to what was, for them, the most important part of the ceremony. As they did, a lone figure could be seen coming toward them from out in the water.

It was Jeff.

Grant Washburn had prevailed on Clark to find a way to make his presence known. To Washburn, it made all the sense in the world. It might even have been necessary for several of the surfers from an emotional point of view. In the weeks that followed the announcement of Clark's termination by MSV, as the surfers talked to one another and tried to decide what to do, one of their first requests—more like a demand, actually—was that Jeff be included as one of the twenty-four invited surfers. For that matter, the guys would have made room for Jeff as a twenty-fifth contestant on event day. Jeff declined before the conversation had a chance to go anywhere. Since the contest's inception, he had never actually competed, even though he was—and remained—among the finest big-wave surfers in the world. Event days had always been, for him, a time to oversee and help, to use his knowledge of the reef and the swells to make the day as near to perfect as it could be. He ran the contest day like an owner or a manager: The event had its judges, its safety personnel, its fans, vendors, surfers, but there was only one Jeff, and it was Jeff's presence that made the day feel like Maverick's and not anything or anyplace else.

This year, Jeff desperately wanted to be included in the goings-on. That part of him was winning out over the part that wanted to flee the scene entirely, maybe jump onto a golf course somewhere and just let the whole thing play itself out on its own. But even as he reckoned with the inexorable draw of Mavs, the real world was intruding. Stripped of the contest directorship, he was pondering legal action, and his attorneys were advising him not do anything that might be construed as lending support to Keir or MSV. That meant no season-opening ceremony on the beach and no appearance at the party that would follow, when the surfers' names would be drawn to establish the heats for that season's contest. Again the corporate side of his life was knifing its way into the part of the world that he treasured most. Jeff was at a loss.

It was Washburn who suggested an alternate route: simply show up at the circle gathering in the water, say a few words to the guys who really mattered in all this, and leave. It wasn't part of the beach spectacle. It wasn't part of the contest draw. These were moments reserved solely for the surfers, the people with whom Jeff wanted to connect in the first place. Grant's suggestion gave Jeff a place to be and something to do, and it gave him an audience with a bunch of guys who wanted to hear from him. Best of all, a few wouldn't see it coming.

As the ceremony went off on the beach, Jeff stood well out

in the channel on his SUP. He did not make his approach until the surfers had completed the paddle-out and were preparing to form their circle. Jeff seemed to appear directly out of the late afternoon sun as it set in the direction they paddled. "Out of the mist," Evan Slater later described his friend's entrance, smiling at the thought.

"Guys," Clark said simply, "I'm glad you're here."

Clark's words were plain, but spoken from his heart. "I want you guys to go get the biggest waves you can," he said. Washburn, sitting on his board halfway around the circle, smiled to himself. He knew that this was exactly what the surfers needed to hear. They needed to know that, despite everything that had happened, Jeff still wanted to see something great go down on contest day. They needed to hear that it wasn't going to be weird or complicated once they pulled on their suits and went out to do what they all loved the best, that Jeff would man up and get through an unhappy situation without any conflict or confrontation on contest day. Jeff mumbled something about all of that behind-the-scenes nonsense, said it should stay on dry land where it belonged. It was the right sentiment. He wished the surfers luck for a great season. And then he was gone, leaving the competitors to talk things over.

"It was perfect," Washburn said. "We're just a big dysfunctional family, anyway. He sort of reinforced that it's okay for us to be that."

The nature of that dysfunction was not fully mature, though; and not long after the spiritual moment with the twenty-four on the water, Jeff was back getting down to the nitty-gritty of scraping together what he felt was rightfully his. The Clark/Maverick's saga was about to take another deep roll underwater.

In January 2010, as the surfers agonized over the missed dates in November and December and strained to dispatch the job that had always been Jeff's, word arrived of Jeff's ultimate response to having the event taken away from him: he was headed to court to try to get his money. His lawsuit against Keir and Mavericks Surf Ventures, filed in San Francisco Superior Court, attempted to portray the dispute in classic surfer-versus-stiff language. Jeff, suing for lost salary and royalties and claiming fraud, was described in the complaint by his attorney as "a passionate and respected member of the international surfing community," while Keir was cast as the leader of "a series of corporations and persons with no interest in surfing other than as a source of corporate and personal profit." In a news release accompanying the filing, Jeff himself was more direct: "I made a mistake and I trusted the wrong people."

Some of Clark's friends got a chuckle out of the characterization, knowing that Jeff had wanted to do business and make money in the first place—hence the deal with Keir to form MSV, and hence the fact that Jeff still held so much of the company's stock. But they had Jeff's back and wanted him to get what he needed in order to move on with his life. The future of the contest itself was imponderable, anyway. For all any of the surfers knew, this could be the last one or it could go on for a hundred years. Outside of maybe Pete Mel and Grant Washburn, no one had much information about sponsorships or corporate underwriting or the behind-the-scenes shenanigans. They were interested enough to be curious, but not enough to invest any time trying to track down the truth. The locals, the San Francisco and Ocean Beach and Half Moon Bay and Santa Cruz surfers—the everyday warriors like Josh Loya and Tyler Smith and Matt Ambrose—would always have Maverick's, contest or no contest. For them, Jeff would always be a presence and a friend. For the rest, the contest either would happen or it wouldn't. If it didn't, they would simply move on to the next great wave, wherever that might be.

About Keir, the surfers had no deeply held personal feelings; Keir was just the guy running a company. Their judgments of him were based strictly on whether he delivered on his promises, and because of his spotty track record with them in the past, they invested little faith in the idea that everything would go smoothly just because he said it would. That was merely business, and it made for easy calculations. If he did a lousy job, they'd just stop coming on contest day and instead surf Mavs the rest of the season, when it was wide open and anyone with a board could ride. If, on the other hand, Keir could pull off a day on which they could get paid for showing up while still honoring the bigger ideals of Maverick's, they would be there—and they would trust Jeff to understand. That was the entire rubric. The lawsuit was extracurricular; it was about people getting theirs. Most of the guys knew Jeff well enough to figure that he wouldn't go down without a fight, and most of them were okay with the lawsuit if it meant Jeff might somehow get back to running the contest itself. Beyond that, they didn't care.

None of the surfers was staying up nights worrying about whether Mavericks Surf Ventures lived or died. To Twig, there was a person like Keir Beadling at every surf contest held everywhere on the planet. If he left, some other guy would take his place. But Jeff Clark was an original, because Jeff invested the vast majority of his time into loving and caring about the surf point itself, and the ocean and conditions that created it, and the idea that these puny humans could find a way to tap just a percentage of all that natural power and beauty and terror. Jeff was still one of us, and Keir would always be one of them.

For his part, Keir had long since made his peace with that divide. He understood the role that he played as a CEO rather than surf guy. He could partition off his own ruthless behavior when it came to running a company or trying to get ahead; he didn't think it defined him as a person, a husband, or a father, and so it became more or less his business flak jacket. As for how he ran Mavericks Surf Ventures, he shrugged off being portrayed as the bad guy by people who didn't know what he spent his time doing every week, or how frantic the scramble was to come up with a record prize purse, or the hundreds of hours it took to lock down myriad other details like the permits for Pillar Point. They'd never know because they didn't care to. Keir was fine with that.

"I never aspired to surf Maverick's," he said. "I also don't think that I *could* surf Maverick's. I don't presume to know what it's like. And most of those guys probably don't presume to know what it's like to run a business. From Jeff's perspective, and probably some other folks, it looks easy."

When it came to Jeff's view of MSV and the corporatization of the contest, Beadling likened Clark's emotional progression to a parent's seeing a child gain his own independence and move away. "The time that Maverick's went off to college was probably a couple of years ago," Keir said, "and now it's on to graduate school and having a life of its own. And that is hard for Jeff as a parent of Maverick's—the original parent."

As for the lawsuit itself, Beadling maintained that the language of their working agreement required them to iron out any differences behind closed doors rather than via legal filings. (Among other things, Clark's news release stated that MSV had canceled a scheduled mediation session with Clark the week before the suit was filed.) In an e-mailed statement to the media, Keir wrote, "It's hard to interpret this as anything other than an ill-advised and clumsy ploy to disrupt the contest season and prevent the competitors and the fans from experiencing a contest. Hopefully, he'll recognize the wisdom of keeping this matter private."

Either way, the relationship was probably headed for a financial settlement with or without a lawsuit. Beadling was already thinking past it. It was the grand plan itself that he wanted to spend his time on, and right now the thing was focused around the 2010 Maverick's Surf Contest, trademark registered.

BY THE EARLY HOURS of February 13, as Chris Bertish tried to grab some rest inside Jeff Clark's condo, most of the checkers for Mavericks Surf Ventures appeared to have moved to the right side of the board. The surfers themselves had finally been able to call the event, albeit not in a unanimous fashion. Needing a majority approval to green-light the contest, they came up with seventeen yes votes after a flurry of Thursday calls, texts, and e-mails—including the passionate missive that Bertish fired from his cell phone before walking onto the jet in Cape Town. It was after Bertish weighed in, but without him actually knowing the result, that the votes came in sufficient numbers to make Saturday a go. The decision afforded Beadling and MSV the two days they needed to get everything in place for the event itself, and for a veritable army of volunteers to begin massing for the jobs they would do on Saturday. These arrangements were absolutely critical because the Harbor Patrol and others weren't pleased about holding the contest on the weekend in the first place, given the nearly 50,000 people who would descend on the area. Beadling needed every one of the forty or forty-two hours he was being given to lock down all the details. Still, the surfers' vote was not a completely clean outcome, nor a fully supported one.

The approval was notable for the quality of its dissent. The no vote was carried by such local Maverick's heavyweights as Matt Ambrose, Shawn Rhodes, and Grant Washburn, guys who surfed the point all season, year in and year out, and who had perhaps the strongest sense of the variables that could make a potentially epic day go haywire. In this case, they had no issue with the prospect of paddling out to meet the predicted 50-foot wave faces. Their concern was with the wind, which was expected to be blowing offshore at a potentially breezy clip, thus knocking down some of the most epic waves or putting the riders in the unhappy position of being blown off the back of such huge curls just as they were attempting to maneuver down the face. But they knew that nobody was going to pay attention to the usual danger signs with $150,000 on the line. *That* was the bigger problem.

More than most, Mark Sponsler acutely missed Jeff's sense of Maverick's during the surfers' discussion and the vote that followed. The two of them had made a very solid team over the years, with Sponsler erring on the conservative side, wanting to deliver to Clark his best guarantee for a great event, and Jeff willing to take a risk and call the contest anyway, based on his overall feeling. It was difficult to imagine anyone else possessing the necessary background to make such a call.

"He just knows the wave," Sponsler said. "I was always more of the meteorology guy, looking at satellite stuff, but if I could tell Jeff that a swell was coming, where it was coming from, he would have a good sense of what it would be like when it reached the break. As much as I've surfed it, I don't know Maverick's like he does. And he has a pretty good sense of when you're going to have a good enough storm, too. He had it all pretty well dialed in. It was intuitive."

When it came to the 2009–10 contest, Sponsler weighed in with his information, which included the forecast for Friday: south to southeast winds blowing over the point almost all day. That forecast stuck in Washburn's head. He and Ambrose and Rhodes all knew from experience that there was often a residual effect from that kind of wind activity. It was just as likely to tear up the waves on Saturday, leaving them choppy and tough to ride. Washburn was advocating setting the contest for a day later, on Sunday, when the wind would have dissipated fully and the swells were still forecast to produce amazing sets. But, of course, one more day of waiting meant one more day in which things could change. In the end the majority of the surfers were unwilling to bet on conditions remaining epic all the way to Sunday. The decision ultimately favored people like Rhodes and Ambrose, and certainly Washburn—people who routinely surfed the point in adverse conditions and knew how to handle its gnarlier side. But Washburn walked away from his phone with an unsettled feeling all the same.

First and foremost, Saturday was going to be huge. Sponsler's forecast suggested as much. The surfers could see it, because so many of them had come to make it their business to follow the weather and wave patterns. But Grant Washburn knew that there was huge and then there was *huge*, and when Maverick's started blowing up like that, it usually brought with it the potential for chaos. Having a bunch of guys gunning for a $50,000 first prize only promised an increase in mayhem. People would be taking chances on Saturday that they might not normally take. They always surfed hard and surfed well, but often there came a point at which the experienced riders would see a huge, unstable wave face, understand how heavy it was about to throw, and decide to pull off and wait for a different ride, a better ride—a safer ride. Not safe, exactly, but safer.

There was absolutely such a thing as too big at Maverick's because of all the other factors involved: the frigid water and the rocks and the hold-downs, to name just three. It wasn't a question of having nerve; it was a question of having sense. All the best riders had that, which explained in part why they were among the twenty-four originally chosen by Jeff some eighteen months prior. But Washburn also knew that even common sense—to say nothing of the finely tuned physical senses that accompanied any venture out to a giant wave— could be overridden by a chance for glory and money, or maybe even simply for a chance at the most insane wave ride ever. It could be incredible Saturday. It also could be tragic.

Grant was not a fatalist, but he was a very experienced realist. He had seen people get trashed by the wave in "ordinary" conditions, seen friends break bones in everyday surf. Right now the riders were so stoked that they weren't going to be in the mood for reasoning. They had waited all winter to call the contest and they weren't going to let this window pass. Washburn, Ambrose, Rhodes, and the four other no voters had no chance of prevailing.

That was all cool, Washburn declared; it was all good. But Maverick's had made a habit of exacting its own toll on the people who tried to take it on when they should know better, and even some of the surfers spoke of the break as if it were a sentient being and not merely a force of nature. Maverick's knew how to punish the ignorant, the arrogant, and the inexperienced, but this time it was also going to be the reverent and respectful veterans who might wind up throwing caution into that south wind.

Grant already knew about himself. He knew that he would find a way to surf the day, no matter what Maverick's threw at him, and walk back out of the water in one piece as he had for years. It was the other guys he worried about. Jeff's absence, the lack of any sort of final arbitration, was built into the new system and the majority had spoken very plainly. Forget the wind and never mind the slop. The big-wave riders wanted to ride.

Chapter 10

*T*HE MORNING ITSELF ARRIVED quickly and without incident. Chris Bertish squeezed off two or three hours of sleep, the sleep that would come to him only after he had visualized himself smoothly traversing the giant face at Maverick's, letting his body go loose and absorbing the bumps and shocks of the churning surf on the way down, navigating that one huge suck-out section, the one that kept wrecking his imagined ride. He woke ready to go. Though by rights he should have been dragging, Chris felt weirdly energized. There were good forces inside him, he was sure of it. He would need all of them.

Everyone at Maverick's understood the consequences of taking to the wave when they either weren't at top energy or lacked their deepest focus. The story of Mark Foo had been told and retold too many times for the true surfers of the

point not to understand. And even if they couldn't be certain
about why things unfolded the way they did, it remained a
cautionary tale. Foo had flown all night from Hawaii to reach
San Francisco with his friend and rival Ken Bradshaw, and in
the hours before they took to the ocean, as they went first to
Doc Renneker's house and then down the Cabrillo Highway
to Maverick's, Foo hunkered down in the back seat of their
rental car, huddled against the cold early morning air. He
looked haggard. He hardly radiated eagerness. Whether that
body language had anything to do with Foo's tragedy was one
of those imponderables. Surfers of all stripes had long been
known to put in crazy travel time in order to reach a particular
swell at a particular location and still soldier through. It was
practically an ethic. Yet the whole sequence of events with Foo
carried an ominous tone. Chris Bertish was hardly the first to
make a grueling trip to Pillar Point, but by almost any standard, the scale of his thirty-six-hour ordeal was off the charts.

Instead of feeling beat up, though, Chris was buzzing.
There was something about the brutality of the trip, the desperation and adrenaline it took just to reach California, that
had set off what felt like a caffeine bomb inside him. If anything, he thought, he might actually need to edge off a little
bit, calm down. He needed to see the wave, read the break.
Half the battle today was going to be simply picking the right
ride and not wasting your time. Each heat lasted forty-five
minutes, and without at least two decent rides you weren't
going to advance to the semifinals. But Chris felt good. He
felt like he could get himself dialed in by the time he had to
make solid decisions. And his legs felt strong underneath him,

which was insane, considering the trip he had just completed. Chris was elated; his positive nature, his sense of constantly wanting to attack the adventure in life, was paying off in a way that he might never have expected. Bertish got up and got rolling, gathering up his gear, shooting around Jeff's living room as if he'd had the longest sleep in the world. His body and emotions were fooling him at top speed. Maybe it could last through the afternoon.

Down in the village of Princeton by the Sea, the morning sun confirmed what first light had merely suggested: the day was perfect and the wind was gone. The predawn fog that had rolled down the Cabrillo Highway and lain on the coast like a thick, damp blanket burned off with surprising quickness, and the local restaurants and bars were abuzz by breakfast time. Earlier, at 5:30 a.m., workers inside the Café Capistrano, a sort of staging area for the food distribution, had quietly preloaded bag lunches and sold hot coffee. Next door at the Old Princeton Landing, a worker came to the front patio, saw the choking throng of people already milling about, and said, "Oh, Lord," before hurrying back in to get the bar ready to open. Just outside, on Capistrano Road, a police officer had pulled up to begin directing traffic; the stubby little blocks of the village already were filling with cars attempting the slow crawl to one of the parking areas. The Half Moon Bay Airport was being used as one such parking lot, with spectators then being shuttled to a drop-off point from which they could begin the walk out to Pillar Point—where, of course, they weren't going to be able to see the contest, whether or not they realized that yet.

That was early. Now, a few hours later, the full scale of the Mavericks Surf Ventures production could be seen: it was wall-to-wall people and things. If 50,000 people had shown up for the 2008 contest, as had been widely reported, then the number today had a chance to exceed that. There was no place for the spectators to go and nothing for them to see with regard to the contest, but they were there all the same.

When it came to the beach and the crowds, Keir Beadling and his company had been walking a fine line for some time. On the one hand, the MSV web site offered a fairly detailed list of ways to see the surf contest without actually being there. For those who felt they had to be there, MSV offered officially sanctioned boat tours and zeppelin rides. The contest webcast, meanwhile, was of high quality, had reached millions of users over the past few years, and now was being broadcast in high definition. MSV had informed multiple media outlets that fans could take to the lawn of AT&T Park in San Francisco, the cool, retro-looking home of the Giants baseball team in the China Basin area of the city, and watch a live feed of the contest on the big screens there in relative comfort—for a $25 fee. A page at the web site, while also hawking day-of-contest T-shirts for $24 and hoodies for $75, quoted Beadling as saying that both options "provide a better viewing experience than the view from the beach."

On the other hand, business was business. MSV had set up the airport parking lot and the shuttle, the more efficiently to deliver people to Pillar Point, and there was no question that Keir's company was prepared for a festival gathering. The advantages of having a huge crowd at the beach on contest day were obvious: any overhead shot of the surf spot would also show a mass of humanity. The image would carry an unmistakable message about the frenzy that surrounded the event. This thing was such a big deal that people would power into a tiny, transportation-constricted area even though they couldn't see a thing. What could be more in-demand than that? When anyone looked at one of those aerial photographs or video clips, they would see all the people and the tents and the scaffolding, the huge speakers and the spectator platform. Anyone looking, that is, would see the spectacle and conclude that something of high value was occurring there. You couldn't call it the Super Bowl of surfing otherwise. And you sure couldn't market an empty beach.

If the sheriffs or the firefighters wanted the beach cleared, they would order it. Otherwise, it was a public setting, give or take, and there was no charge for anyone who wanted to make the journey out to the point. Keir knew from experience that thousands and thousands of people would want to do just that, if for no other reason than to say they did. On some levels, he thought, it would be irresponsible—and certainly bad for the brand—to have nothing awaiting them when they arrived.

To Keir, that was the point. The point was for people to see "Maverick's" printed on the front of a shirt or the side of a pair of sunglasses, and for them to immediately connect that with a way of life and an ethos, more than any single event or sense of place. Keir had seen that marketing strategy executed effectively. He thought the Maverick's brand could be bigger than Hollister, but done right, without any obvious sellout connotations. He wanted his products first moving through surf shops and outdoors stores, gaining credibility with core buyers, and only then moving on to the mega-malls. He didn't want Maverick's shirts jammed onto the sale rack at JC Penney to start. The idea was to remain pure in the core consumers' eyes, while eventually hoovering major-league money out of newbies' wallets. It was no mean feat.

Maverick's was a wave, a surf point, a story, a spirit. The surfers knew the word to mean all of those things. Beadling, a Duke graduate with a Case Western law degree, had a company whose mission was to take the name Maverick's and morph it into a moneymaker. He believed that there was such a thing as being true to the basic history of the place and still turning a profit. In reality, his company had been so close to broke so often that "cash-poor" had come to feel like standard operating procedure. But maybe today was the day that everything turned.

As he walked toward the charter boat that would take him and three dozen photographers and journalists out to sea, Beadling was struck by the thought that, for him, there wasn't anything left to do. The contest was ready. The weather looked promising to the point of perfection. By any measure, the amount of media coverage and exposure leading up to this year's event was the greatest in the history of Maverick's—some of the coverage good, some of it bad, plenty of it steeped in the recent unpleasantness, but all of it directly referencing the event, the spot, and, however perversely, the brand.

Without a fresh infusion of cash, MSV was going to have a hell of a time paying its bills come Monday, but Beadling was not naturally inclined to panic. The contest was going to be fabulous, and surely it would renew sponsors' interests in being aligned with Maverick's and MSV. With the sponsors would come new money that could be used to take care of the current debts. And if enough new money came in, Beadling would be able to seed the coming year's plans; he could find the path to financial solvency that he had been searching for since the early 2000s.

No one had the slightest idea how much time and effort he had devoted to keeping the thing afloat and Beadling felt quite sure that it didn't matter. The surfers wanted a contest done right; the vendors wanted to get paid; the sponsors wanted to know what their money was getting them. No one wanted details. The details fell to him.

Keir stepped onto the charter that would take his observation group a half mile out, just off the right shoulder of Maverick's. The boat's captain came aft for a quick conversation. "I've been doing this a long time," the captain said, nodding toward the choppy water that lay just beyond the harbor. "Once we get into the open ocean today, I want you to keep one hand on the rails at all times. We are going to be rockin' and rollin', and we're going to be pitching pretty good over the swells, so there will be a lot of motion going on. If you're going to be sick, be sick over the side of the boat. If you fall overboard, wait for the next Jet Ski to come by and pick you up. If you see somebody else go overboard, don't take your eyes off him. And if your camera goes overboard, wave it goodbye."

Keir glanced at his BlackBerry; if he could get a cell signal

at sea and could stay upright long enough to type, he'd probably be able to bang out some Tweets and send a few photos
to the Maverick's Twitter account in real time. The big circus
on dry land was all handled, basically. The executives and
their families had a place to go and be seen on contest day.
The MSV crew had even set up an area for the competitors'
friends and families. Keir was headed into the open water to
actually see the creature that he and his company had spent
the past two years trying to keep alive and thriving.

Jeff Clark, meanwhile, stood on a figurative island. Despite
the remarkable power and confidence he still radiated when
on the water, Clark arrived at contest day without a role. It
was disorienting for the surfers to see Clark puttering around
without anything to do. The local papers already had written
their stories about Jeff's lawsuit. When a reporter from the
Santa Cruz Sentinel asked him a few days earlier for an update
on what was happening, Jeff replied succinctly, "The classic
squeezeout." It made for good copy no matter how much it
oversimplified the truth, and it was every bit as polarizing as
Clark intended it to be.

But now it was the day itself. The words and the lawsuits
had been left on dry land. All the fun, all the danger, all the
adventure lay out in the water. And the irony was, at this
precise moment in history, Jeff Clark didn't have any place
else where he honestly wanted to be. His friends had seen
that coming. Sitting one afternoon a few weeks earlier at a
beach bar, one of them said, "So much of him doesn't want to
be out there during the contest this year. But the rest of him
just can't do it. The waves are out there, and the event, and

his buddies. There's no way they're going to keep him away. And there's no way that he's going to be able to keep himself away. So there you go."

And so on Saturday, rooted on by his wetsuited friends, Jeff Clark hopped on a Jet Ski and headed out of the harbor, past the jetty and toward Maverick's. Clark could tell that the fog would lift, as if to open the curtain on the point that he had called home for thirty-five years now. Everything about Jeff's life as a surfer told him he had to be there. He *knew* the place. He could help if things went bad.

Jeff bobbed off to the side of the wave's shoulder, ready to caddy for a friend or rescue someone in trouble. He would also have a front-row seat in case history happened. The ultimate insider was playing the role of designated outsider for one day, but everybody at Maverick's understood that he should be there—that it wouldn't be a great Maverick's day if he weren't. The rambling, dysfunctional family of big-wave surfing was gathered once again.

THE 2009–10 MAVERICK'S SURF Contest began with remarkably placid conditions on land and a riot out at sea. The dissenting surfers from earlier in the week had seen their concerns about the wind dissipate for the most part. There was almost no breeze left by the morning, meaning the riders would have a fair shot once they tried to stand up and get down the face of the wave. But anyone who would describe the surf as glassy smooth that day was getting it dead wrong. Friday's offshore breeze had indeed left its mark. There was a bit of residual choppiness to be found in almost every wave that blew up off Pillar Point, with the water churning and moving around in different directions. The waves were breaking huge and unpredictably, often arriving in quick, spiked sets. Massive quantities of water were on the move seemingly everywhere.

Still, the overall confluence of factors was stunning: it was going to be sunny and brilliant all around the wave, and yet massive and dark and cold inside it. Mavs had broken big before, but never like this on a contest day. That the rules required the surfers to paddle into the wave, not get towed into it like in so many other instances, lent the event an air of uniqueness and valor. This was a big-boy exam. There were potentially historic rides to be had, with giant rewards to the victors. Maverick's, as always, was going to demand its cut of the action.

As he made his way to the beach at Pillar Point, Chris slipped on his headphones and began pumping music into his brain, getting a rhythm going, setting himself up for the pounding rides that were to come. He was ready to smile. He was ready to charge. His ten-year quest had finally come to this: he was about to surf the Maverick's contest. He no longer cared about the details of his trip, his missing gear, his bereft bank account. At this point, he would have bodysurfed the wave just to be able to say he'd finally made it into the contest lineup. Chris's heart was full. He intended to soak in every drop of the experience.

He got a faceful. As Chris rounded the corner at the point, all hell appeared to be breaking loose. Like Grant Washburn moments before him, Bertish was nearly stopped in his tracks by the sheer enormity of the commercial sideshow that had overtaken the beach. By now, Chris had surfed Maverick's enough times on non-contest days to have a basic sense of how things looked, sounded, and felt when they were normal. This was not it. He blinked hard and pushed his earbuds in a little tighter, thinking that perhaps he could just hang out for a few minutes, let the music and the rhythm sink in, find his game-day focus, and then head out. Though Grant had already made his way, Chris didn't want to be in the water yet. It was still a good while until their heat began. If he could pass some of the time here at the beach, even amidst this over-the-top setting, so much the better.

IT WAS NOT A rogue wave that took out the beach and the stuff on it and the people standing there. "Rogue wave" means something else entirely in the context of open-sea calamity. In the days that followed February 13, the term got thrown around indiscriminately, evidently for want of a better way to describe what happened. But the physics of the situation were actually fairly simple: the waves were huge, and their might was not exhausted simply by their forming barrels and crashing down into the deep water bowl out at the Maverick's point. They would continue to roll, to form whitewash like a rushing river of salt water steaming toward the breakers and the beach beyond. They had not yet expended all their energy.

Out on the charter, Keir Beadling's BlackBerry began

buzzing and humming to life not long after the boat got into position near the surf point. At first, the texts were terse and incomplete: Water was washing out the beach. A wave jumped the wall. Lots of people were down. There might be some injuries. It took Beadling a while to begin piecing together exactly what had happened.

The same set of conditions that had created massive waves out on the surf point was sending them hurtling toward land, and in the case of Pillar Point, all that stood between the wave and the beach was a low-slung jetty built many years earlier by the Army Corps of Engineers. That much was predictable, but the scale was not. Generally, the jetty did a serviceable job of breaking up the surges before they plowed into the beach. Not today.

Today, the water was coming in with such force, and moving around at so many different angles, that the smartest move anyone could make was away from it. But the thing about the Super Bowl is that, on game day, most of the people tailgating are also the ones who know the least about the sport. So it was on the beach, as well. Despite incursions from smaller waves in the previous hour, and despite the obvious implications of a monster day, dozens of people had decided to stand on the seawall, trying vainly to get a glimpse of the early contest heats being run half a mile away. Chris Bertish looked to the jetty in utter astonishment. Clearly, these people had never, ever been to Maverick's.

Danger aside, what they were attempting was hopeless. Even from the upper angles of the bluff above the sand, which only a few dozen people could access, the view was terrible.

Even if you caught a glimpse of one of the surfers in his brightly colored contest jersey, your vision could be immediately obscured by another wave breaking closer to shore. It was like having another person walk in front of the television. Put it together with the salt spray and mist, the glare of the sunshine off the water, and the morning was essentially one giant, colorful blur.

It did not deter the rookie crowd from heading for the jetty. The seawall itself rose above an area of craggy rocks and reef, not the forgiving sand of the nearby beach, but no one seemed to notice or care about that either. Washburn paddled out a few minutes before Chris came to the beach, and Grant could already see the force of the water, could see that powerful waves would soon be crashing at the feet of the seawall and peppering anything beyond it with jet blasts of water. Those rolling, grinding breakers out at Maverick's—the ones that picked up and dumped surfers like specks of lint—would explode into forward-racing whitewater, and the whitewater had to go somewhere.

High tide was due at about 10 a.m., but even now, still well before nine, it was clear that some serious mess was headed right where the densest throng of humanity had gathered. Washburn had already warned the cameramen and vendors he knew. He had told the sponsors to hightail it. He had made sure his own family was not coming to the "family area." The people he had tried to warn all smiled and nodded, but Grant knew full well that most of them weren't going to leave. Reluctantly, he finally told himself to get on with his part in the show, and get out there on the water like he was supposed to. Grant walked his board into the surf and was gone. A few minutes later, Chris Bertish, earbuds tucked and music pulsing inside his head, came around the corner and saw the whole spectacle unfold before him.

A *LITTLE AFTER* 8:30 in the morning, Twiggy Baker, surfing in the first heat of the day, saw a massive swell approaching, went paddling hard for it, and got the drop just in time. As he started to carve down the face of the wave, the water wall suddenly appeared to double in size; the thing just picked itself up and sucked out half the ocean at its feet as it rose taller and taller. It was like falling down a mine shaft. Twiggy started working furiously to reposition and survive. Using all his experience at Mavs, Twiggy stomped down on his board, keeping it in physical contact with the face. He made it down with his grinding rail, and he shot out toward the right shoulder before the thing collapsed and heaved over on him. Twig was still upright for another 50 yards or so before the whitewash caught up to him and blew him off his ride, but he had enough to help him get out of the first heat of the day and advance to the semifinals. Flea Virostko, surfing more conservatively than anyone could remember but using all of his hard-earned Mavs knowledge, made the most of his chances and scored two decent rides; he was going to join Twig in the semis. Popular Hawaiian surfer Dave Wassel got through, too, with a couple of hard-fought rides. But there was no doubt about the conditions: they were overtly hostile.

Already, with the contest just beginning, several riders

were pulling off waves just as they were poised to take off. The surfers could see that the break was going to be ridiculously big, simply unrideable. It felt as though any chance taken was going to be punished—and indeed it might be. As time wound down in that same first heat, Half Moon Bay veteran Ion Banner, knowing he needed a good ride to advance, took a shot on a dramatically rising wall that his own long experience at Maverick's would normally tell him to avoid. Banner's ride was over quickly; he took a spectacular ten-foot free fall down the face, his board cartwheeling through the morning spray, and then was buried under the wave that slammed down on him. When Banner finally came up after a pounding in the spin cycle, he had a bloody nose, a swollen eye, bruises up and down his body, and no points.

CHRIS WAS VISUALLY LOST, his brain in soft focus, staring off at the horizon line, when the sudden blur of activity on the sand brought him back to where he was. He looked toward the jetty and saw bodies sprawling on the rocks below. Water was blasting over the wall. Chris knew immediately that a wave of incredible strength must have jumped the jetty. Of course it had. It had slammed in directly from the surf point. God, it must have come angling straight toward those people. Why hadn't they moved? What the hell was going on out here today?

But even in that eyeblink, Chris realized that Maverick's wasn't done yet. The wave had barely broken stride in jumping the wall and now it was headed for the beach. Scaffolding came down, the tall metal legs of the stands knocked out from underneath by the magnificent force of the water. Chris could see loudspeakers and equipment that had been set up for the broadcast and the post-contest award ceremony; the stuff already had been washed over and now was being dragged out to sea. Vendors' tents, food areas, the "family" zone for competitors—everything was getting blasted. Chris began to consider the worst. He frantically scanned beach-line as the water began to recede. Was anyone down? Were there people being swept out?

"It just came out of nowhere and wiped us all out," a woman would later tell reporters as she bled from the hand and knee. That was how most of the spectators felt: it had been some freak accident. The people lined up on the sea-wall either had no inkling that they were putting themselves in danger, or else they had made conscious decisions to be there anyway. The California Department of Forestry and Fire Protection had certainly understood the danger; the agency had dispatched extra personnel to start clearing the beach and moving fans away from potential trouble. But the support crew didn't make it until after the fact. Instead of cautioning people and moving them to safer ground, they spent their time putting people into splints and bandaging their wounds.

Chris, clad in his wetsuit, broke into a run toward the injury zone. Already he could see people with broken bones, bloodied hands and faces, twisted knees and ankles. He could see, in the shallows, the remnants of everyday lives being washed to sea: wallets, iPhones, cameras, backpacks, sunglasses. There were laptops and pieces of electronic equipment floating there, ruined immediately by contact with the salt water.

Chris homed in on what he could do to help. He put a young spectator over one shoulder and helped another woman limp off the rocks, and he guided them toward the south end of the beach, the farthest point away from the impact area. It was controlled mayhem. People who hadn't been hurt were tending to those who had, and of course the folks on the jetty had taken the worst beatings. More than a dozen of those standing on the wall were pounded onto the rocks below. Three of them ultimately were taken to hospital for more serious injuries. The rest, a total of thirteen by official count that rose to the level of being significant, were dealt with at the scene: fractures, bloody scrapes, bruises, contusions.

At least forty people were knocked off their feet, including some who were standing on the beach—not the seawall, but the beach itself—when the wave hit. Pillar Point was turned into a flood zone in the span of about ten seconds, swamping the spectators who were still standing and changing the atmosphere from festive and up-tempo to a state of emergency in the same amount of time. It was emblematic of the raw power that was at play in the ocean that day, but it was bad news for the event itself. The attention had suddenly been diverted from the surfers to the fans, and that was never a good thing.

"We were very lucky that nobody was swept out to sea," said Scott Jalbert, the CDF battalion chief who rushed to the scene. "It's a force of nature that can't be predicted."

Out on the charter boat, Keir's BlackBerry slowly brought confirmation of what was happening. He could do nothing;

the boat was not going to return to the harbor until the conclusion of the contest, hours and hours away. Keir began receiving text requests for comment as the CEO of Mavericks Surf Ventures and thus the highest-ranking spokesman affiliated with the event. But he couldn't see what was happening, had no idea what the full scope of the damage was, and certainly wasn't involved in the care of those who'd been hurt. That was out of his hands, and thus out of MSV's hands. It belonged to the sheriff's department and the firefighters.

Was MSV liable for what happened to those spectators? There were signs posted at the beach warning people of the danger of incoming waves. Keir's company had said several times that there were better places to watch the surf contest than from Pillar Point, even as it also told people where to park and how to get to Maverick's itself. Either way, there wasn't much legal restriction on a public beach. Keir's company certainly didn't own it, and furthermore it wasn't even entirely clear who was responsible for the beach itself as opposed to the seawall or the bluff above it. Entities ranging from San Mateo County to the Harbor District to the Air Force to the Corps of Engineers all had a hand. Mavericks Surf Ventures had received a permit from the Harbor Commission to host the event in conjunction and coordination with these agencies. The rest, including any immediate notion of ultimate responsibility, was unknown.

Keir's phone pinged with an incoming call. He steadied himself against one rail of the charter, which was pitching dramatically in the huge swells, and strained to hear what was being said. Keir listened for a moment. "I'm sure it's being blown out of proportion," he finally replied. "We're all having to deal with Mother Nature. Everybody has to exercise common sense."

The comment would return to haunt Keir, because the words looked so severe and out-of-place once they were put into print. For that matter, Beadling was going to wind up spending some time trying to explain what he meant by "common sense" when about half the stuff that got washed out to sea was directly related to MSV: spectator bleachers, the awards stand, equipment. But in the moment, on the boat, his words were spoken without malice. He didn't yet know the extent of the calamity on shore—it was all dribs and drabs, text by text, as it filtered out to him. You had to see the scene to understand what was really happening, and Keir could no more easily do that than the beachgoers could see the surf contest.

Back on the beach, Chris Bertish stood in the aftermath, with people still sprawled about and T-shirts floating off to oblivion, while other folks tried to right some of the tables and shade structures that had been knocked down. He was perhaps an hour away from surfing the Maverick's contest for the first time in his life. He had already done what he could on the beach, and the good vibe that had accompanied him as he rounded the corner at Pillar Point was long gone. He had to try to get it back.

Chris pulled out his cell phone and punched up a familiar number. Jeff Clark answered. Clark motored in, picked up Chris, and took him back out to the contest site. Bertish had made his call: He was going to spend the entire heat before his on the water, away from the human commotion. He was going to get back to staring at the wave and trying to read the action, to feel it a little bit. His margin for error was thin, even by his hard-charging standards. A mistake today was going to hurt more than usual. Chris knew that there was nothing more important, in that moment, than to give himself every possible chance to succeed.

Chapter 11

*T*HE GREAT IRONY OF WHAT HAP-
pened later was that Bertish
wasn't tempting fate. Considering
how often he had been known to do just that—it was practically his big-wave calling card over the years—you'd think
that if Chris got into trouble, it would be because he had gone
flirting with it again. But that wasn't the case at all. In fact,
Chris already had caught his first wave of the day, and he had
done so without any of the normal Bertish stuff. He really
hadn't gone banzai down the face of a screamer that he knew
would eat him. Maybe, in the end, it was just plain bad luck.

His first ride had been a "good-enough" wave—an easy
enough break to access, and Bertish had set up and pulled in
without much difficulty. He calmly traversed the face to get to
the bottom, drew his line, and surfed out without incident and
without fireworks—a solid, if unspectacular, performance.

Chris knew he couldn't advance out of his heat without at least a couple of well-scored rides, so to have one on the books was a good first step. He could now head back out and try to land a big one, secure in the knowledge that he had a set of points already established and enough time to make a few more attempts. He would need a solid ride, because his heat was stacked with talent. Of course, so was every heat in the contest.

Virtually all of The 24 had been waiting for two years since first learning that Jeff Clark had included them on the list back in the summer of 2008, for the contest that never ran. Back then, it was Clark making all the decisions about who was in, who was out, and who was an alternate; and although the surfers themselves would be loath to rank the first dozen names on any big-wave list as necessarily much better than, say, the third dozen, there was little argument about any of the riders picked by Jeff. All the credentials were solid gold.

The heats themselves were drawn in a fittingly random manner, with the contestants' names written on ping-pong balls during the pre-season party and pulled out one by one into a bracket. The first six ping-pong balls comprised the first heat, the second six the second, and so on. That was it. Competitively, the riders either surfed their ways through to the semifinals or they lost on the spot. And if a certain heat was filled with great surfers—well, why wouldn't it be? Each time out, a surfer needed to have better rides than other surfers in his heat. That was all. If you surfed well when it was your time, then you were likely to move on. You had the same chance at the same waves as the people you were competing against—or, as most of the big-wave riders would express it, competing with.

"Mavs is different," one surfer said. "Just getting out of the water in one piece is a good thing. That's what is so cool about the sport—the camaraderie and respect. Everyone knows that you could have a good day or a bad day, and you could catch a great wave or see a great wave go by in someone else's heat. But if you lose and it's ultimately about how the ping-pong balls came up at the party, that's cool. It's still all about your heat."

Bertish's heat included Shawn Rhodes, the respected thirty-nine-year-old owner of the NorCal surf shop in Pacifica. Rhodes was the kind of surfer who would head to Mavs on a day when most of the rest of the world was backing away. Jamie Sterling, a brilliant rider from Hawaii, was in the heat, and Washburn, too. Washburn, despite never having won the contest, had an uncanny ability to get out of the first round and into the semifinals (and often the finals) year after year. Grant simply knew how to pick a great wave, surf it, and survive to surf another one after that. It was a skill earned through years of trial and error and scars.

Chris understood that he needed to be terrific, sooner rather than later, if he were to advance to the semifinals and buoy his chances of being invited back for next year's contest. Generally speaking, the defending semifinalists had a great edge on gaining a bid the following year, and dead broke or not, Bertish planned on at least getting the invite. Maybe he could figure out a way to finance one more trip back to California somehow. Ten or twelve months was enough time to come up with Plan B, Plan C, or Plan X. At any rate, that was all well down the road. He was here right now. Considering everything he'd been through, this was a success in its own right. Now he wanted more.

Chris paddled back out from that first ride and then began to wait, watching the waves on the horizon line. The sun had burned off the lowest-hanging clouds, leaving streaks of white high overhead and some cotton balls piled up against the hills to the east. It was a long paddle. The surfers were sitting easily 150 yards beyond the usual lineup area because the waves were breaking big and deep.

Though he was satisfied with his early ride, Chris realized it was only one score. Chris had already seen Grant get a couple of clean, nearly perfect rides; it looked like Washburn hadn't even gotten his hair wet. Ryan Seelbach had scored at least one terrific wave, and Shawn Rhodes was lurking out there. Chris didn't feel anxious, exactly, but he needed to get another wave as efficiently as possible. As much as Chris loved soul surfing, he was exactly the kind of person who could get up for a contest—and he wanted at least to make this one count for something. They were offering a prize, so he was going to try to win it.

Chris looked for his opening. Out on the horizon, he saw a massive swell forming. The other surfers either didn't see it or weren't in a position to do anything about it, and Chris initially had the same thought—it wasn't going to be his wave. He began to paddle for it, but, glancing back toward land, he quickly realized how far out he already was. There was no way, he figured, that the wave would do anything other than roll under him as it set up for a massive detonation closer to shore. On most days at Mavs, he would have been right.

On this day, as Chris watched in increasing amazement, that distant wave suddenly grew a full body. It began to heave wildly, building itself four stories tall as it seized up and prepared to throw forward. In that instant Chris recognized it for the beast it was. The wave appeared to have drawn virtually the entire ocean up into it, and it was breaking in a place that Mavs waves never break. If there had been time to consider it, perhaps Chris would have marveled to himself. Even an old hand at big-wave surfing could be impressed by the sheer magnitude of things from time to time. It was like surfing history.

There wasn't time to admire because in that same moment, Chris could see that what lay between that massive, dark green barrel and the reef was him. This wave was going to break right on top of him. He had essentially paddled himself into an explosion. Chris took off, scratching hard, his heart racing. From off to the side, Grant Washburn looked over and saw Bertish's orange jersey in the water, bobbing furiously with each stroke. Grant could see that Chris had chosen the only option really left to him: head directly for the wave, hope to duck under it just as it broke, and perhaps come out the other side in time to grab a saving breath. And what Washburn could also see, as the wave threw and prepared to close out, was that his friend wasn't going to come close to getting that done. This force was going to crush anything in its path. Chris was one such thing.

Chris paddled toward the wave, going as hard as he could. But the thing had broken already; it was throwing over the top with overwhelming force. Chris hunkered down on his board and tried to duck through it. The gray-green barrel rolled over on him as it thundered down and spiked into the ocean below. The sound was of a train coming through the living room.

THERE WAS NO IMMEDIATE commotion about Chris Bertish disappearing under the wave, because, only four heats into the contest, it was already a day of epic cleanouts at Maverick's. Surfers all over the place were coming up gasping for air and spitting blood and checking ripped wetsuits and throwing up, then heading back out to face the monster again.

Beyond all that, the people who spent time surfing with Chris had always known him to be willing to charge a wave when the odds said not to go—and to somehow come out the other side with his ass intact. Even big-wave colleagues couldn't believe some of the shit he ate on the water without quitting or giving in. Chris had always seen as challenges the kinds of waves that other experienced riders would call bad risk, as opposed to acceptable risk. Chris had the reputation among his peers as someone who would pull into any wave at any time, and while he wore the mantle proudly, he also was surrounded by friends who urged him to find some saner path to the great adventure.

"I tried several times to get him to tone it down a little, but he's a Cape Town surfer," said Gary Linden, a surf veteran and head judge for many of the world's most prestigious big-wave events. Linden offered the words as a full explanation. Bertish had earned his big-gun stripes on the jagged cold waves and massive throws at Dungeons, among other South African surf posts. In fact, if the story of big-wave surfing were told accurately, Bertish's name would start showing up in the very early chapters, because he was included among the first groups of real chargers at Dungeons. At about ten years old, Chris started putting boards in the water, keeping up with his brothers and indulging a ferocious competitive streak that already had emerged. Bertish tried all sports, but quickly found that if he wasn't in the water, he wasn't fully engaged. By his teens, he was testing his mettle on larger and larger waves, and eventually he made the passage out to sea, to take on Dungeons with a like-minded group of pioneers.

Like Maverick's, Dungeons was a place that simply could not be surfed by the casual rider. You were either all in or you didn't bother. "Picture a deep, dark, kelp-infested, cold-water spot, three miles from anywhere," Chris once explained. "No roads. You can only get there by boat, out in the ocean, off a huge seal colony and home to some of the largest great whites on the globe. Now that's before you even start talking about the wave! Dungeons is definitely one of the scariest, thickest, most unpredictable and powerful waves on the planet."

Of course, that was precisely what lured Chris out there: the danger, the adrenaline, the rush. In a culture that knew its share of drug users, Bertish got his kicks clean. He drank moderately, didn't smoke at all. His only craving, he once said, was for "big, nasty waves." Critically, Chris also believed in the value of fear. It had become, over the years, a part of his worldview, as espoused on his web site, chrisbertish.com. And Chris really did live by the words he posted there: "Dream big, play big." "Enjoy, travel, explore." "Go out of your comfort zone to achieve beyond what you once thought possible." "Ignore people who think small, the ones who tell you why something cannot be done." As for fear and big-wave surfing, Bertish accepted them as ready partners. To him, the question was never whether fear would surface, but how he would find a way to put that emotion to good use.

"Everybody gets scared in big-wave surf," he wrote on his site. "You have to use it to your advantage. Never hesitate. Hesitation will cause your worst nightmares to become a reality!"

It was an approach that made for hairy—and historic—rides. Bertish was the first person to paddle into one of the massive waves at Jaws on Maui, a break that almost everyone thought impossible to surf without a tow-in. He was also the first to win the coveted Billabong XXL Paddle award, for the largest paddle-in wave ride of the year, during the 2000–01 season. He set the United Kingdom surf world on its ear in 2004 by paddling into the Cribber off Cornwall, a reef formation near Newquay that produces 30- and 40-foot waves under the right conditions; and he was among the first to paddle into waves at Ghost Tree, the tricky, difficult spot just off Pebble Beach where Peter Davi died.

Chris had an outsized appetite for the risk-and-reward mechanics of big-wave surfing in large part because the system fit his general approach to life. He had always surfed for the sheer push of getting on the board and finding out what might happen. He was committed to chasing the biggest waves he could, wherever in the world the search might take him. He also had long since come to terms with the realization that, like most surfers, his love for the sport and the brotherhood was going to have to be enough. Though he certainly hadn't set out to find somebody to pay for his passion, it had not escaped Chris's notice that there were surfers getting paid enough to offset some, or even most, of their costs. While he was globally recognized as an elite practitioner of big-wave riding and was invited to almost every competition, Bertish had experienced little in the way of sponsorship. After a while, he got down to openly soliciting on his web site—and even, sometimes, on the face of his surfboard itself—for companies that might be interested in throwing a few bucks his way. It was never anywhere near enough.

What he had left was his surfing, the pure love of the sport and the water. These were the elements which sustained him. He loved the risk and the adrenaline and the feeling of getting on top of a massive breaker, maybe getting barreled. One of his Cape Town buddies remembered a day when Bertish got ready to stand up on a ludicrous wave at Dungeons, one that was going to rag-doll anyone silly enough to try to ride it.

"You'll never make it!" the surfer shouted to Bertish.

"I know!" Chris screamed back, a huge smile across his face. He proceeded to charge.

This day at Maverick's was not like that, exactly. No one was taking random, pointless chances. There was nothing for The 24 to prove, certainly. But the day was without question about risk. Waves were breaking in places so far out that very few people could remember the last time anything like it happened without a tow, yet the money and the glory of the contest day dictated that chances would be taken way out there, and also close in, and at every point between. And the surfers all knew, because they had to know it by now, that Maverick's almost never let anyone off the hook without a fight. The physics didn't allow it.

The 50-foot barrel that broke on top of Chris, as he desperately tried to swim his way past it, was an almost perfect example of how the local reef formation could concentrate and redirect the energy of a wave that had traveled thousands of miles to reach it. It was a wave so broad, so powerful, that even the approaching front edge of that reef-ramp was enough to cause it to begin to concentrate. Chris saw the effect when he looked to the horizon and realized with a start that the thing had started to build. All of his experience at Maverick's told him that the wave wasn't going to break out there, no matter what his eyes appeared to be telling him.

As Chris went hard toward the break, he heard a thunderous crack overhead; everything around him became shadowed. He took a huge breath and braced himself. The force of the impact immediately drove Chris into frigid depths, and disorientation began almost immediately. He felt himself being spun, pushed, kicked, pulled. His body was getting yanked in multiple directions at once, dragged backward through the water—backward, or was it sideways? He was being spun to the point of not being able to tell. It was a common experience among big-wave surfers, not being able to discern up from down, but now Chris didn't know if he was traveling toward the rocks or away from them. He could not find the surface of the water. The vision was gauzy in one direction, fully black everywhere else. But there was no thinking, no calculating. Chris simply had to stay alive.

Up on the surface the rescue sleds began to work the whitewash, waiting for Bertish to pop back up so they could blast in and get him. Every one of the Jet Ski drivers that day already had plunged into hazardous conditions to rescue surfers from further pummeling by the waves. But there was no early sign of Chris. Pinned under the crushing weight of the waves, held down for a second time, he simply couldn't find up. He was being hurtled toward the Boneyard at high speed.

And then Chris began to feel it. He could feel the haziness closing in around him. Things settled down into a lazy slow motion. He could sense himself growing calmer. Right there in the middle of the spin, his world was now moving in quarter-time. It was a peaceful feeling that came over him, a sense that he didn't have to worry so much, that it was going to be okay. It was familiar, soothing even. It was familiar because Chris had felt it before and knew what it meant: he was close to blacking out.

As the rescue teams began working more furiously, crisscrossing the water at top speed and kicking up plumes of spray, their collective tension started to ratchet. This wasn't a case of no one having seen something awful happen; Chris was plainly visible when he got smashed and taken under. But there was nothing on the surface to work with. No one could even find Chris's signature Jeff Clark surfboard. Suddenly it was several Jet Skis, not just a couple, that were roving the infield searching for a sign. Out on Keir Beadling's charter boat, someone said it out loud: "They can't find Bertish." As it happened, Bertish was trying to find himself.

In the middle of his roll, Chris knew. He began to fight the sense of calm, to kick for some adrenaline somewhere. He fumbled around for the leash of his surfboard and located it, and he could feel that it was not snagged on anything under the water that would hold him down. He had gotten pasted, yes, but he was not trapped. He was simply messed up. He tried to focus. It was no choice, really; he had to start moving in some direction. Chris chose the direction of the most chaos and began to struggle toward it. The air was almost gone from his lungs, but he could see the place where the water was turning a lighter color. Chris knew from the stories of other riders that so many of them had been fooled into thinking they were swimming the right direction when in fact they were heading deeper into the ocean. But he had to go for it. It was his last best effort.

He found the light and followed it. His chest, arms, and legs were on fire. The light became brighter. It was no longer blackness around him. Chris saw what appeared to be a rim of gold. It felt like he was about to see God, like the universe was opening up. He swam and fought the rising panic. When he burst all the way through, the sky above him was the bluest blue he had seen in his life. It was brilliant, shimmering, shocking to his eyes. It was his favorite color ever. He gasped and hacked and spit, all seemingly at once. He was somehow past the worst of the whitewash, or maybe only blessedly between waves; his body had been dragged hundreds of yards beyond the impact zone. Chris took a full, ragged breath and looked around, bobbing there in the water, nearly lifeless. He was going to need help.

The rescue sled operator was on him in what seemed like milliseconds. He dragged Chris onto the sled and powered him away from the danger before another set could pound them both. Chris groggily looked around him and realized he had come within a very few washes of the Boneyard. He laid his head down on the sled, motionless. He tried not to pass out.

"Do you want to go to the paramedics?" the driver asked.

Chris did not answer. He had nothing left. He couldn't even summon the energy to speak. The driver asked again, and then a third time. Chris lay on the sled without moving. He knew he was finished and that his next move should be to shore. He had done it, after all. Bertish had finally made a wave in the Maverick's contest, ten years after he started trying to. There was no shame in going now. But as Chris lay there panting, his heart rate slowly coming back down, his cobwebbed mind began to drift. Chris operated on the principle of positive thought, but he was scratching hard right now trying to come up with something beyond his basic relief at having survived. He loved to compete, but this was serious stuff out here. Chris needed to find something to hold on to emotionally, because physically he was tapped out.

He let his mind go. Suddenly, he was back in Cape Town. He could see his late father's office, and inside the office there was a picture hanging on one wall, the illustration that his father had always kept around for inspiration and a chuckle. It had been his dad's favorite. What was that image? Chris thought. He lay in his exhaustion and his pain and he focused on the image. Slowly, it formed.

The picture was one of those motivational posters that seemed to be for sale at every store in the mall, the kind with a glossy photo or cartoon and some inspirational phrase or other. This one was a drawing of a stork trying to swallow a frog. The frog was about halfway down the stork's gullet, but the frog's arms were still sticking out of the stork's beak, and he had them wrapped around the stork's throat, trying to choke it out. As Chris remembered it, the caption underneath the picture read, "Don't EVER give up."

It had always been Chris's favorite picture, too. At his core, Chris believed everything about it. He believed in corny sayings, things that others might toss off as dime-store wisdom. He had the evidence of his own life as proof that those clichés weren't worthless. He had lived by several of them, and he had a world of experience and adventure and friendship and achievement to show for it. When he wrote on his web site, "There is no such word as Can't or Impossible," he meant it. Chris had never entered into any phase of his life with anything other than full belief, full commitment, total respect and enthusiasm. This is what he wrote: "The universe likes people who are different, who are out there looking for possibilities, making things happen, making the most out of life, who are determined to achieve and succeed." He believed it, all the time. Chris never had to be talked into going for it. He wasn't going to be talked out of it this time.

"I'm good," he sputtered to the driver.

"What's that?"

"Take me back out."

When the driver got him close enough, Chris slid back into the water, got on his Jeff Clark board, and paddled back toward the men in his heat. His determination was pure. Every surfer in this contest had suffered through his share of crappy, stomach-twisting, limb-thrashing hold-downs over the years. Every guy had been afraid at one point or another, or deeply wounded, or humiliated, or broken. And every one of them eventually wound up right back here, surfing with his friends and peers, trying to figure out what the primal force was all about and how to touch it. It was the only place most of them thought they might have the slightest chance of unlocking any of the universe's tumblers. It was what they did. It was their articulation of the world. It was what *he* did.

Chris looked at his watch; his heat had about four minutes remaining. At the very least, he told himself, he would still be on the water when his part in the contest was over. He lay on his board and paddled. The worst that could happen was that he would end his Maverick's experience beside his peers, a small satisfaction over being towed to some first-aid station. It might have to do.

But as Chris scanned the horizon, his expression changed. Against every odds imaginable, a wave was forming out there, right at that moment, and most of the other guys were too far out of position to even try for it. Incredibly, almost stupidly, the wave was rolling in at a perfect angle and with just the right speed for Bertish to catch it. The damned thing was going to break exactly where he already sat.

Chris couldn't believe his luck. He took a couple of strokes into position and was able to drop right in and catch the wave cleanly. It was almost like his first ride, a no-frills wave that nevertheless broke plenty big and delivered a nice face for him to glide down. He descended the wall, set the rail hard to the right, and made it out the side. This time, at the end of the ride, Chris didn't even paddle back out. He'd gotten his two waves, survived a Maverick's heat, and turned in enough rides to record a real score. It was the achievement he needed. This time, he really was done.

Except that he wasn't. When the scores were tallied and the results announced, Chris Bertish was moving on to the next round. His second wave had been enough, just enough. Grant Washburn won the heat with a commanding score and Ryan Seelbach advanced as well, but Bertish's last-gasp ride, that magical wave that appeared just before the air-horn sounded to end the heat, had given him the points to advance to the semifinals.

It was absurd. It made no sense. Chris smiled to himself and then laughed; he ought to be glad just to be alive. And he was glad. He just wasn't finished. The frog was still bringing the fight.

Chapter 12

BY THE TIME THE SEMIFINALS rolled around, it was well apparent that what was happening at Maverick's was both extraordinary and inscrutable. The outsized wave faces were one thing, but the water was churning and moving in ways that were alien even to longtime regulars. In the early heats, Twiggy Baker caught an incredible ride down a 50-foot face then got blasted off his board by whitewash from the closing barrel. Flea advanced to the semis, but not before taking a horrible mid-face wipeout and barely escaping serious injury. In the first round, Greg Long, with his massive résumé of big-wave success, had sat maybe 50 yards outside the rest of his group in the lineup, banking on the knowledge he had gleaned from his early-morning venture out to see his brother and others take to the wave. But Greg caught only one ride, and when the wave closed in on him it pushed him down with such force he actually bumped the ocean floor—maybe 50 or 60 feet underwater—before he scrambled back to the surface.

Mostly, though, it was the surfers' own sense of occasion that lifted the day above all expectations. They were scaling heights that had never been achieved by paddle-in surfers. Gary Linden, situated on the bluff above the point with the rest of the judging crew, blinked several times in surprise and made a note to himself to go back and check the photos and video images later. He wasn't sure he could trust his eyes, because they were looking at 60-foot waves. He wasn't sure if any of the biggest ones had been successfully ridden, but there was no doubt in his mind about a few of the clean-out sets—they were 60s. Kenny "Skindog" Collins, a man who had surfed the point so often and so well over the past decade that he would make any shortlist for a Maverick's Mount Rushmore, would later stand before his friends and say, "I don't think I could ever say I caught a big wave after seeing what you guys did today. You took it to a level that I only dreamed about." That was after Collins made the finals.

It was weird, unlikely, unknowable surfing. Men stood at the top of waves they had never before considered rid-ing, and as often as not they pulled away at the last second, astonished at the risk they had almost taken. At one point, Grant Washburn got right to the lip of a huge-breaking wave and looked down. He could see the bowl curling up under him like an onionskin piece of paper lit by a match. All of his experience, all those years of quiet sessions with nobody watching, usually told him very clearly the odds of success at Mavs; and this time, in these conditions, it hit Grant that he had "maybe a 1 percent chance of coming out of that wave." At the last instant he turned off, and as he did the huge force felt as though it kicked itself out from underneath him, throwing itself forward with a vicious strength. It was mayhem inside the wave, the water churning and sucking out all up and down the face, with ridges and fissures everywhere. It was a horrible, grinding, life-sucking barrel. Grant had cost himself a ride, but saved everything else that was important.

In the first semifinal heat, Twiggy Baker reminded everyone why he was such a presence on the international scene—and in the same heat, he also reminded them why Maverick's was one of the most unpredictable forces on earth. Early on, Twiggy caught a monster wave, went slicing down the side after an exquisite drop, and floated his way through the curl, pushing out in front of the whitewater blast for a football field or more before he was finally overtaken. It was a thing of beauty, exactly the right mix of guts and skill. It was why the sponsor companies had finally lined up behind Twiggy and given him money to circle the globe with Greg Long searching for the next big wave. Twig's ride earned a perfect ten from the judges, the only such score of the day. But this was Maverick's. Through the remainder of the heat, Twig looked on in increasing dismay as the second wave he hoped for failed to materialize. Incredibly, when the horn sounded time, Twiggy had a score for only the one ride. His day was brilliant, but it was also now over. With Greg Long having gone out in the first round, the previous two Mavs champions were officially eliminated. A new winner would be crowned Saturday.

Flea too came up short, with no scores in his second heat that could advance him. The great Peter Mel, for whom a title was wished by his peers probably more than anyone else, did not score enough to move on. Grant Washburn, for all his experience, came up almost bone-dry in the semis, never getting anywhere near the kind of wave he would need to reach the finals.

But Anthony Tashnick, who in 2005 became the first person besides Flea Virostko ever to win at Maverick's, caught a very nice first wave, surfed it in one piece, and made it through to the finals. Dave Wassel got a bomb, and he and Shane Desmond, each in the middle of a gargantuan day, found their way through, too. And no one was taking things to the brink like Carlos Burle. Burle apparently had made the decision, early in the day, that he simply was going to charge every wave in sight. He was a madman on his board, willing to trade hideous wipeouts for a couple of epic rides. As the crowd in the channel cheered and pumped fists, Burle went for wave after wave, getting absolutely thrashed in the process. But when the semifinal heats were done, the Brazilian also had gutted out just enough huge rides to rack up the points that vaulted him into the finals. There wasn't a person on the water who disagreed with that score. Burle was raising the bar, knowing full well that one of his peers might then be inspired to try to raise it again.

Skindog Collins, all skill and balls, had no problem with any of that. Skinny, as he was often called, summoned all his

Mavs knowledge to find his way down the side of several liquid mountains. Burle was one of his best friends, and Collins gleefully accepted the challenge that he knew Carlos was throwing down. Though he would later declare that he had ridden only modest waves, everyone who knew Skinny knew better. The Santa Cruz native had once again found his way through, and that made five finalists. One spot remained.

By the time he got back out on the water for his semifinal, Chris Bertish no longer had designs on anything. He was happy to be alive and on a board. Sitting in the lineup of the second heat, he felt pure elation. He was still here. He had come this far and refused to quit, and now he was at this great place, with all these people watching, surrounded by talented surfers and lifelong friends. In almost every significant way, Chris had gotten what he came for. This was the reason he flew, to be here now. As competitive as he was, as much as he loved to win, Chris was willing to take this moment and call the day a victory. It was not the same as saying he was finished.

Chris waited. He felt calm now, patient. The worst had come and gone, and the wave had not taken him. Just the opposite: it had set Chris free. He no longer felt like an incomplete surfer. He had made it to the Maverick's contest, had taken one of the worst beatings of his life, and here he was, still on the water, still connected. All that was left, really, was to find that next ride, do it one more time. It felt like a celebration more than a contest. It was the feeling that Chris always chased on the water, and it was so, so good.

The wave that he was looking for arrived as if by appointment, and it came from way, way out. Chris had seen it on the horizon and watched it rapidly approach, and this time he was already in position, out of the danger area and situated in the drop zone. If that wave broke, it would be his to ride, and Chris wanted to take the thing from as close to the top as he possibly could. He started from well in the back of the lineup, very deep, and he stayed near the back of the wave as it formed and prepared to throw, waiting just a bit longer than usual to begin paddling for the drop. It was worth trying to ride. Chris stomped on his board and started to cut down the face, and as he did he glimpsed the far section of the wave opening up ahead of him, toward the right shoulder. He realized that the wall of water had a chance to be something special.

Chris pulled in hard and hugged the side of the water wall just as the wave threw slightly over, and he made his call: he was willing to take the hit if it meant going inside that barrel for just a while. He tucked in tight along the inside wall; the green of the water grew lighter very briefly as it reached its apex over his head and caught the afternoon sun. It grew taller, more dramatic; the thing practically yawned as Chris sliced through it, giving him that tiny little glimpse of the pure stuff. It was a barrel like surfers everywhere have been chasing since the sport began, only it was bigger, almost supernatural. It pulsed with the energy of life. The experience was like driving a bus through a collapsing tunnel; all the wonder of surfing was caught in that one powerful curl. Chris, on several levels lucky to be there at all, savored every second. He felt himself inside nature. *This* was why he had come. It was why he had wanted to try in the first place.

When he got through and heard the whoops and the roars

of the people in the water, Chris knew it had been enough. *He* was enough. He could have paddled in at that point, flown back to Cape Town, and been satisfied with the result. But the wave was not yet finished with him. When the six finalists were announced, Chris Bertish's name was among them. For Chris, one more adventure remained to undertake. And for Maverick's, it meant that the long afternoon was about to move toward its more surreal edges.

GRANT WASHBURN'S THEORY ABOUT hideous travel, and how it relates to surfing the giants, was as good an explanation as any for what happened in the late afternoon hours off Pillar Point.

Washburn was a veteran of such things. He had traveled to South Africa several times, always hoping to surf Dungeons and often having to wait out the slow days and the nonstarters in order to finally get a taste of the greatness. On those travels he met people like Twiggy Baker and Chris Bertish and gained the perspective of one who is willing to chase these forces, chase the high that the big-wave guys could feel only when they were riding giants. Grant had waited through more than one unproductive visit to South Africa before finally getting his chance at Dungeons. He knew about the desperate longing for the wave.

"You take the thirty-hour or the thirty-five-hour trip, and by the time you get there you are just on such a mission," said Washburn. "And it's a vicious journey. It's just so long. The mental fortitude that it takes to get through that—and then you finally hit the water, the thing you've been trying so hard to get to. You get there, and no matter what the conditions are, you're saying to yourself, 'Did I make this whole trip just to sit here and not paddle for one?' No. No way. You're going."

Washburn reflected for a moment. "In Chris's case, you add to that the fact that he has been trying to get into the Maverick's contest for so long . . . I just don't know that we can compete with that kind of intensity. That's another level, you know?"

The final round of the 2009–10 Maverick's Surf Contest went off amid rapidly changing conditions and shifting tides. The rides were no longer automatic. They were there, but the positioning that had worked earlier in the day wasn't going to be right now; it was as if the rules of only an hour or two before didn't apply anymore. The tide, so full in the morning, was going lower, and the waves were beginning to shoot across the reef with such speed that they were hard to catch.

The air was heavy with salt spray, accomplishment, and history. Only the salt spray could be seen coming; everything else happened practically when no one was looking. In this case, the history arrived in between the semis and the finals. The downtime, conceived in order to give the finalists a chance to regroup, offered a small window of opportunity for the rest of the big-wave world to take a crack at Maverick's on contest day. Guys with world-class credentials who nevertheless hadn't broken into The 24, people like Shane Dorian and Mark Healy and young charger Shawn Dollar, had been sitting all morning, awaiting their turn. It was too good a day to simply stay in the channel and watch.

Grant hadn't bothered going in after his semifinal heat

because he knew that he had not made it to the finals. He was in no hurry to leave the water. So when the surfers headed for the lineup, they dragged Washburn with them, still wearing his contest jersey. It turned out that Washburn was being given a front-row seat to the show.

A few minutes into the mini-session, Shawn Dollar stood up at the top of what everyone immediately realized was going to be an astoundingly huge wave. The thing just kept growing, kept rising; you could feel the power in the water. Dollar, all energy and spirit, somehow skittered to the foot of the beast, his magnificent drop accentuated by the fact that the wave was literally still building as he was surfing it. Shawn should have been destroyed about a hundred times on the way down, but he somehow stayed up. Eventually, the whitewash powered him into salt and sand, but not before he had gotten his money's worth. Later in the day, it would be said that Shawn had paddled into a wave that conservatively measured 57 feet on its face. Washburn, having sat right by it as it happened, knew it was at least a 60-footer. Either way, it was thought to be the largest wave ever paddled into at Mavs.

In the eyes of many, there was almost no way that the final could top any of the things that had already occurred on a day that was practically cartoonish in intensity. When the contest's last act got under way, anyone watching could tell that Maverick's, as it always did, had come to collect the bill that was due. Fatigue was beginning to set in for the surfers, and that alone carried a significant risk.

Carlos Burle, enduring wipeout after wipeout, caught a bucking bronco of a wave early in the championship session and paid for it in pain and deep bruising; thrashed and spun through the impact zone nearly to the rocks, Burle finally surfaced, threw up, and promptly paddled back out to try another ride. Dave Wassel got a nice wave, and Tashnick caught a decent ride. But as the time counted down, both guys were having trouble finding a second one. Only Shane Desmond seemed to be in a good position; he very quickly notched two nice scores, and then went looking for a bomb that might put him on top.

Chris Bertish had no idea about any of that. All he knew, because he saw it happen, was that Wassel and Tashnick had had good rides, and that Carlos was surfing like a madman. By Chris's count, Carlos had already caught at least a couple of great waves. And Chris knew that he had passed on his own first opportunity, about twenty minutes into the forty-five-minute final, when he looked down a 15-foot drop and noticed a huge section of the water that appeared to be swirling and churning. Poised on the lip, Chris sensed that the wave was about to take on entirely different characteristics. At the last second he pulled off and let it go. As he did, that 15-foot face began to rise as if on a hydraulic lift, adding 25 feet to the inside of the wave. The drop would have been catastrophic, far too steep to navigate. It was the right choice for Chris, because the wave likely would have meant a body-slam into the wet cement and the end of his day. Still, it meant that he had zero rides so far. He needed to stand up on top of *something*.

About ten minutes later, Bertish saw a swell moving toward him rapidly and in good position, and he caught it and rode it exactly as he would have wanted. If you didn't know anything about the place or the wave, you'd almost call the transaction routine. But Chris made it down cleanly and had a nice bottom turn and got out without incident, which qualified it as a very solid ride. He was quite certain he needed another one.

What Bertish didn't know was that Carlos Burle's theatrics, while mind-blowing, didn't leave him in first place as Chris had guessed. Burle was attempting some incredible waves but taking terrible falls. He was actually being marked down because he was only getting about halfway down the face before eating it. The mantra among the judges, especially the respected Gary Linden, was always that risk equals reward—but only to a point. You still had to surf the wave if you wanted a score. Burle was getting the holy hell beaten out of him—earning the respect of every other guy in the water that day—but, in the end, he was not scoring significant contest points.

All Bertish knew was that he had time to try for at least one more wave. Chris figured that if he could score a nice ride, he had a decent shot at finishing in third or fourth place, and that prize money alone might be enough to allow him to pay back his brother and friend. He tried to stay loose. He could feel his body beginning to shut down physically, the cold water taking its toll on his tightening muscles. Compounded by three days of travel mayhem, exhaustion was right around the corner. His neoprene wetsuit felt heavy; he noticed for the first time all day how constricted he was inside it. He needed only enough willpower to complete another ride or two. Chris began to focus again on that poster in his father's office. Where was the frog now?

When the next big set came, Bertish was ready. As a wave came frothing up, Chris scrambled to his feet and stood to go. He got over the top ledge of the water wall and began the descent. He had made it about halfway down the churning face before he saw what was actually opening up beneath him.

It was the bump.

This was, to be precise, the exact bump that he had seen in his mind's eye the night before, at Jeff Clark's condo. It was the bump that he couldn't navigate for the longest time in his vision, the one that would suck out and create a huge disturbance in the wave. It was going to get nasty and stay there. In that instant, Chris flashed back to how he had solved the problem the night before: he had to go rubbery, stay flexible. His body was worn out and he was stiff on the board, but if he stayed that way there was no way he could get past this lump in the water. Elasticity was all.

The roar of water around him was deafening. Chris compressed his focus. He was descending directly toward that lump—of course he was. It was as he had dreamed it. When he finally slammed into the bump, he hit it square on top; there was nowhere else for him to go. It was time.

Chris suddenly went soft, right at the point of contact. He let his legs and knees absorb the blows like human shocks. The jolt reverberated all the way up his legs and through his thighs and his board rattled under his feet. He could feel the wave fighting him, the water moving every which way. Chris refused to fight back. He relaxed his body again and again over the bumps, forcing the board back down just enough to maintain contact with the water.

And then, just like that, he was past it. He was past the bump and headed for the bottom in one piece, and then he made that bottom turn and got a few more seconds' worth of paradise at the foot of this monster, her magnificent power crackling and thundering over his head. From the boats idling off the shoulder of the wave came a roar of recognition: Bertish had done it. He had stood up yet again on this magnificent, malevolent day.

Just after that, the wave detonated behind him and blasted Chris forward off his board in a whitewater explosion, plunging him under and holding him down there as two more waves crashed on his head. A rescue sled twice tried to get to him, but the runner couldn't make the save before a wall of water cracked him. The turbulence below the surface was absurdly violent. Chris could feel the energy seeping out of him; his adrenaline was used. It was no time to screw around. When the Jet Ski came for a third pass, Chris summoned everything he had, released the leash on his board rather than risk having it drag him off the sled, and lunged for a handle. His Jeff Clark special was now officially on its own. The driver expertly loaded Chris and dashed off to the side. Chris, once again, was being hauled to a safer place while he tried to find his bearings. He had no idea that he had just won the Maverick's Surf Contest.

Chris felt a strange taste in his mouth; it was blood. Somewhere in the intensity of the wipeout, his lower teeth had punched all the way through his lip. He got off the sled a few minutes later and, after taking a minute to gather himself, reached for a second, backup board which he had long ago stored at Jeff's place and had dragged out with him for emergency use today. It seemed crazy, but there was still time left in the heat, and Chris was so disoriented that he couldn't think of anything else to do. He began a slow paddle-out toward the breakers, but he never made it to the lineup before the horn sounded to end the contest. That turn of events, in the end, was his saving grace.

What Chris had forgotten was that months ago, during his last visit to Clark's condo, he had taken the screws out of that board to use them in another. As soon as he had begun paddling out Saturday, his screwless, unsecured fins had dropped out of the board and sunk to the ocean floor. Unbeknownst to him or anyone else, Chris had been heading toward some of the nastiest waves in Maverick's history on nothing but an unguided, albeit well-shaped, plank. It would have been a calamity. Instead, it was another great story. Maybe someday they would put that on a poster and hang it in an office.

AT THE AWARDS CEREMONY Saturday night, every element of the Maverick's story was on display—the "big dysfunctional family" of which Grant Washburn often spoke. Everybody involved with the contest itself—surfers, judges, rescue teams—was still in a state of elevated shock over what had been accomplished. It was, by acclaim, the greatest day of paddle-in surfing in the history of big waves, and that was a history that took in some incredible moments at Waimea, among other astounding locales. The scale was, even in the immediate aftermath, difficult to comprehend. "The stuff I saw today just blows my mind," Dave Wassel said. "We erased fifty years of surfing in one day."

As the drinks flowed and the volume increased, other aspects of the story came into view. It was impossible, of course, not to notice that the ceremony was being held inside a conference room at the Oceano Hotel and Spa rather than outdoors, a reminder that the decision to throw everything onto the beach during a weekend with guaranteed tidal surges had necessitated more than one change of plans. At one end of the room, the contestants and the other surfers, a massive big-wave brotherhood, hooted and slapped backs and threw down drinks. Bottles were passed and passed again. Nearby, a throng of people surrounded a man, powerful of build, his dark hair generously speckled through with gray. As he stood there, enclosed by a circle of big-wave riders and friends, Jeff Clark, the man without a contest, had to have known that he was home.

The awards presentation itself was ragged. All the materials had been washed out to sea or otherwise ruined. What remained was the banner that had been used to hand-write, in felt-tip marker, the names of the contestants as they advanced through their heats. Made of thick black material with a Maverick's logo and white slots onto which the names were scrawled, the banner resisted attempts to anchor it securely against the wall of the conference room. It finally was hung crookedly in a makeshift rope-and-bungee operation. The second semifinal listed one of the contestants as "Chris Burtish."

Still, the sentiment was real. The day had been exactly this epic. Carlos Burle, beaten and sore, spent a few minutes trying to figure out how he could not have won when he had taken such obscene risks to challenge the biggest waves, but he also said, "I'm super happy. The whole scene was something we could leave behind as a lesson for the next generation, for whatever is coming next. We all went for the next level. We all went for that."

It was not without a price. Bruce Jenkins, in his column the next morning, noted that at least half a dozen surfers— a quarter of the field—were either "injured, dazed or rendered temporarily lifeless by interminable hold-downs." The miracle, on such a huge day, was actually that no one was seriously hurt. Burle took three terrible wipeouts; Bertish had his moment; Flea's air-drop was one for the ages. And for every wave well ridden, there appeared to be another five or six that went haywire in one way or another. The surfers themselves appeared overwhelmed by what had happened, what they had done.

Gary Linden told the assembled mass that the waves were the biggest he had ever seen anyone paddle into, "and I'm sixty years old." And he took some time to speak about Cape Town, South Africa. "My favorite place in the world," Linden said. "The people are the most gracious, kind, cultured, hard-charging—and this guy, Chris Bertish, represented Cape Town today."

When Chris stepped up to receive the ceremonial $50,000

winner's check, he was sailing. He certainly knew where he was, knew what he was doing, but the rest of it played out in a dream state. Bertish had nothing left inside him physically, yet he felt filled. A warm glow of accomplishment radiated from him as he told and retold his story to clusters of surf writers who knew him well and to local reporters who had never heard of him. He dedicated the victory to his father and "to anybody who has ever had a dream, a passion. I've been coming back for ten years trying to make my dream come true. When I was hurting out there, I thought that in life you sometimes only get one chance to live your dreams. I put my head down and went back out."

Chris posed for photos with all of the finalists, each of whom was greeted by a thundering ovation. Almost every man thanked Jeff Clark by name. When Dave Wassel was presented with the Jay Moriarity Award as the person who best exemplified the spirit of the late surfer, Wassel's humility shone and he struggled for the right words before finally saying, "I hope that everybody remembers Jay the way we do, as a true sportsman, a true waterman, a guy who just put his head down and went, because he knew that it was the right thing to do."

It was the right sentiment on the right day. It had been a day of going for it, pushing boundaries. Now, standing in the middle of the raucous conference room, Keir Beadling surveyed the scene and took it in like a proud parent. "I'm in shock," Beadling said. "I feel like I just saw ten years into the future of big-wave surfing. I just couldn't believe what they were doing." As he spoke, Beadling stood a few feet away from Clark, the two of them in separate orbits and yet still connected by the event, by the legalities, by mutual relationships, and by their history. For a night, all of that would find a way to coexist peacefully. There was no drama; the family got along. It wouldn't be for a few more weeks, in fact, that the ground under their feet began its shift.

Chapter 13

THE IMMEDIATE AFTERMATH OF THE surf contest was twofold: profound international disbelief at the height of the waves that were successfully ridden by surfers using only the power of their paddling arms; and intense local and regional debate over whose fault it was that the event was marred by the ugly beach scene.

On the latter count, nothing approaching unanimity was forthcoming. Keir reiterated, several times, Mavericks Surf Ventures' essential position that it was not responsible for the actions of the people on the beach in choosing to be there. Beadling did, however, speak of the need for MSV to consider what steps it could take to ensure that something like that didn't happen the following year, most likely by working with the different agencies involved to draw up new event guidelines. "Maybe we block the beach off altogether and push everyone back further," he said. "Maybe we spend more time showing people what we can do online with the webcast, since we had more than a million people on the webcast that day. I would imagine we will be taking steps for next year. I just don't yet know what they are."

None of the entities involved acknowledged outright ownership of the thin strip of land that constituted the beach at Pillar Point. San Mateo County officials checked right after the incident and found that the county did not own the land. Their records indicated that the Harbor District owned the beach, and the State of California the bluff above it. The Harbor District said that its records showed the breakwater was owned by the Army Corps of Engineers, and the beach by the Air Force. The Air Force replied that, according to its documents, its ownership of property ended at the cliff above. The Corps of Engineers said that no one had contacted it about the contest, and that it would never have granted permission for anyone or any structure to be placed on the jetty. The sand itself, site of the big washout, essentially went unclaimed. Partly because of the general confusion, none of the people injured at the event had made any noises about suing. Maybe they just didn't know who to go after.

Chris Bertish returned to a hero's welcome in Cape Town, a riotous celebration at the airport organized by his brothers and his girlfriend. The turnaround, for Chris, had been predictably brutal, no matter how thrilling the weekend. The morning after the contest, Valentine's Day, he was sitting in the terminal of the San Francisco International Airport, waiting to begin his long journey home. He was still fuzzy-headed from the all-night party at the Oceano in Half Moon Bay, but Chris couldn't afford to sleep in. By the time he got home, it would be Monday. He needed to get back into his office, get on the road, and go see some of his clients. Although at that moment he was still utterly broke, he also had a chit that he could play with a little bit: $50,000 American coming to him via check from Mavericks Surf Ventures. He could pay off his brother and his friends, get back level, and even put some food on the table and a little rent fuel in the bank account.

Back in Cape Town, the check did not show up immediately. Chris chalked it up to the usual post-event runaround. He hadn't expected the money to be waiting for him at his hotel, after all; that wasn't how things were normally handled. Chris spent his early days at home tending to his business, hanging with his friends, celebrating the victory, doing interviews, and reveling in the feeling that everything he had ever said he believed in had come back and honored him. There was talk of a book project, maybe even a movie based on his story.

The surfers themselves, meanwhile, were about to confirm an essential truth: that for all of the chatter about the largest prize purse ever offered in a big-wave event and the "Super Bowl" of Maverick's, most of the people involved would surf it or any other great wave for free, anytime it broke, and on whatever notice was given to them to make it. Most of them usually did anyway. In early March, less than two weeks after the 2010 Maverick's contest rewrote the book on big-wave surfing, the call suddenly rang out from the top surfers and from organizer Gary Linden: the Todos Santos event in Mexico, the first ever, was a go.

Todos Santos, a tantalizing reef break several miles off the coast of Ensenada, was famous for its deep turquoise water color and its solid, clean slabs of ocean, tremendous wave faces of 40 feet and beyond. Most of the guys had found a way to surf it every season. This year, Linden was spearheading an effort to make Todos part of a sort of semi-official big-wave tour, as it was such a regular spot in the rotation for most of the guys. Predictably, perhaps, the surfers were immediately ready to say yes. Greg Long and Twiggy made it there, and Pete Mel, and Grant Washburn and Carlos Burle. Halfway around the world, Chris Bertish got the call from Greg Long, immediately summoned his brother to work the flights for him, and took off from South Africa yet again, this time borrowing another bit of cash in order to travel thirty-four hours to San Diego, drive across the border (and another four hours south) with Jeff Clark, set up his boards, sleep for two and a half hours, and then hop on one of the boats headed out to the reef in the predawn morning.

In the end, Mark Healy, the popular Hawaiian who had been an alternate at Maverick's and was among the group that surfed the near 60-foot killers during the break between the semifinals and finals that day, was crowned the winner at Todos Santos. Healy's day was filled with huge rides, a result that his fellow competitors found fitting. Healy charged into the waves because he was a hard-charger, because it was the way he felt the closest to the wave, to get after it and try to get inside and get barreled and see what happened. He took some audacious gambles, courted serious physical risks, and somehow emerged not only unscathed, but with the title of champion.

His grand prize for winning the first Todos Santos event: a bottle of tequila.

"No money and no press," one contestant said. "They went on their own and paid for it themselves. It should answer the question of whether surfers are greedy, you know?"

It was becoming apparent, comment by comment, that more of the Maverick's crew were bothered by the talk of money than were energized by it. As much as the surfers were happy to chase a prize and a check, it had begun to annoy several of them that the Mavs contest Jeff Clark founded now appeared to be driven by money, by sponsorship, by vendor booths and hoodie sales. Those elements were always going to be in play at any contest, but this felt more like the tail wagging the dog. For the longest time, guys like Long and Twiggy and Skindog Collins had been able to divorce themselves from most of those conversations on the grounds that it was Jeff's thing to deal with; he had made his bed and invited a corporate element into it in the first place, starting back with Quiksilver. But Jeff's firing as contest director had changed the dynamic, and now the veterans were in the middle of those conversations. They knew more about the machinery of Maverick's than they ever had known before. And with each increase in their knowledge, their esteem for the idea of the contest as it was currently configured waned just a bit more.

They weren't alone. Down in Silicon Valley, the co-founder of Barracuda Networks, Michael Perone, wrestled with an upcoming decision that was his to make—whether to put even more money into the Maverick's Surf Contest. It wasn't strictly about the dollar figures; Barracuda had money to spend on sports tie-ins for its branding. But Perone's firm already had invested $150,000, receiving a 10 percent stake in Keir's company, and now Barracuda had the option to buy another 10 percent for another $150,000. Keir needed the cash infusion in order to pay his bills from the contest, but Barracuda's participation was not guaranteed.

One sticking point was that Barracuda, like many of the sponsors, had signed on with MSV under the impression that Clark was a vital and integral part of the operation. Instead, Jeff was fired, and the event itself felt ragged and poorly executed in terms of the public relations and marketing opportunities. The scene on the beach was chaotic; the awards ceremony was washed out; the presentation at the hotel had the feel of the makeshift operation that it was. The banner showing the event scores was hanging sideways along the wall. Companies like Barracuda could not be blamed if they were disinclined to sink more money into a venture that might make them look bad by association. In this case, Perone made his decision: he wasn't going to be exercising that purchase option. But he was going to reach out to a few of the surfers individually, people like Skindog Collins and Pete Mel and Shane Desmond, to let them know where things stood.

Keir had been counting on the opposite outcome. He was expecting, he said in an interview months later, for companies like Barracuda to be "converting promises to obligations, from receivables to payables" for MSV. He thought Perone would raise Barracuda's stake in MSV and inject the operation with cash. Instead, Keir's company did not have the cash flow to pay even some of the smaller bills that were associated with the production of the contest. And Chris Bertish's $50,000 prize was certainly going to have to wait.

Keir went into a mode of hyperactivity, meeting with potential investors and renewing ties with existing sponsors, beating the bushes for cash. He had to come up with some operating capital. But as February rolled into March, then April, then May, some bills continued to go unpaid. The broadcast crew had been largely unpaid. It was something of a pattern. Mark Sponsler's deal with MSV called for him to be compensated a modest $50 per month to consult on weather and wave issues; he went months at one point without receiving a check. Linden was owed a small retainer. There were water patrol operators and others who were due money, but there was no money to pay.

Months after his life-changing victory, Chris Bertish received a partial payment from MSV on the monies owed him, with the rest promised down the road. The other surfers eventually were paid, too, either their winnings or their appearance fee, the one that Keir had waived back in 2006 to such acute disapproval. But the veterans, like Mel and Washburn, were sensitive to the notion that the surfers were getting money while the people who actually worked the event were still short. "It reflects on us, too," Washburn said. "If we get the prize money but then seem like we don't care that all the other guys who worked on the contest got defrauded, you know, that's not cool. You gotta pay everybody. And not only did you not pay everybody, but you didn't pay the judge and the weatherman, who are the only two people in that group that we surf with. So you didn't even pay those most closely related to the surfers."

Washburn was beside himself, his emotion no doubt furthered by his own frustrating past with Beadling. He exchanged e-mails with Katherine Kelly Clark, whose response was essentially that MSV was clearly going through a rough time, but it was about to turn the corner. She, too, realized that the money wasn't there, but Katherine's position when it came to the contest was absolute: she wanted the thing held every year because she believed it good for her community. When the notion at one point was raised of simply skipping the event for a year to see if it forced a change in the way things were organized and managed, Katherine was one of the first to vocally oppose it. To her mind, in a tanking economy, the last thing anyone ought to be thinking about was boycotting a moneymaker for the community.

But Keir was grinding. The weeks went by. He rationalized the shortfall by telling himself that companies all across the U.S. were going through similar hard times, but it didn't change the facts. He was at times not paying himself a salary at all. For a contest that had been going on for a decade, and one that Keir's company had controlled since 2003, there was remarkably little left to market, and nothing to bank. It was mostly intellectual property, really. And because the company was cash-strapped, it couldn't capitalize on what was, by acclaim, the greatest day in the history of paddle-in big-wave surfing. There was no financial backing to put together a DVD, no money to produce a show for Fuel TV or anyone else. Keir was just trying to keep the lights on at the office.

And then, in the span of just a couple of weeks in the late spring, two astonishing things happened. First, Keir Beadling and MSV ran into someone who was actively interested in giving them the kind of money that could change their entire outlook. At almost exactly the same time, the foundation of the contest began to crumble beneath them.

The money came from a gamer who had found a way to make his interests pay. Legion Enterprises CEO Mike Sepso was the co-founder of an absurdly successful venture called Major League Gaming, which, true to its name, had taken the idea of people playing video games against each other and turned it into a mega-million-dollar pro league. Sepso earlier had made millions in the broadband content and delivery industry, and he then turned his passion for online gaming into a full-fledged business. Legion-controlled company Major League Gaming, based in New York, had since 2002 conducted pro video-game tournaments all around North America, and Sepso and his partner got them televised, webcasted, delivered to mobile devices—the works. It was a success built significantly on Sepso's ability to put together sponsors, advertisers, and clients. He was great at it. He now wanted to consider whether he could be great at synergizing something else.

When Sepso looked at the Maverick's Surf Contest, he saw a product that was incredibly appealing. The problem lay in the execution. The event was undersubscribed by sponsors and advertisers and the like. Sepso wasn't a surfer—but, then, he didn't have the slightest inclination to go treading into the surfers' areas of expertise. He thought that there might be a way to use his marketing skills to take the Maverick's contest—and eventually all of the big-wave contests around the globe, stitched together in a true Big Wave League of some kind—and turn it into a sponsored bonanza. When Sepso looked at what Keir Beadling was offering, a chunk of the company with an option to buy a controlling interest, he saw seed money well spent. Sepso had $350,000 to give; it was, to him, nothing more than an exploratory run at the company to see what was there. Keir, after months of scrounging around, was finally going to be able to make payments and begin the long, drawn-out process of mending fences with the vendors he'd been forced to stiff since February.

MSV still had the contest, and now it had money with which to offset some of its mounting costs. But what Mike Sepso did not know, because Keir Beadling didn't know it either, was that the contest itself was about to undergo a challenge.

Not long after the 2009–10 event was over, while Keir was trying to gather enough sponsorship to pay his bills, Grant Washburn began receiving a series of phone calls and texts. The message, from other surfers and from some of those in the business community, confirmed the thought that Grant had been turning over in his mind for months: the opportunity existed for an entirely new way of approaching the contest. What if the surfers took over the operation themselves? They would come up with their own sponsor money. They would determine on their own when to hold the contest, which they already knew how to do, since they had just done it for Keir. They would invoke the spirit of the way their friend Jeff Clark had always called the event, toning down the total prize purse if that felt necessary, but more importantly re-establishing that the surf came first and the commercial aspects last. They could return the thing to its roots as a celebration of the wave, not of a brand. And they would have Washburn, along with Peter Mel and several others, at the forefront of that effort.

All of the feedback he received told Washburn the same thing: the surfers were ready. But they needed someone to run the point, and to people like Greg Long, the answer was obvious: it needed to be Grant, or Grant and Pete together, because they were the true guardians of the surf point. They were the locals. They could make it their business to tend to the ongoing interests of the contest, not to mention the spot in general, because in dozens of little ways this was what they were already doing. Long and several other surfers told Grant it was time for him to come forward, to take the next step.

Washburn hesitated. The last year or so, in which he had been asked to ferry information and concerns back and forth between Keir and the surfers and also to referee the Beadling–Clark squabble, had left a mark on him. And he certainly hadn't run a contest or tried to organize anything as inherently scattered as a global group of surfers. On the other hand, Washburn had to admit to himself that he had been one of those who was growing unhappy with the direction of the contest, the corporatization of the thing. This was a chance to move the other way, even if only just a bit. He had to be willing to back up his words.

Grant thought about it. He talked it over with other surfers, and he spoke at length with his longtime friend Mel. Pete told him that he would stand with him. The surfers told the two of them that they would, too. And when Michael Perone and Barracuda Networks entered the picture as a potential sponsor of the newly formed group, the idea began to look more like a reality.

The news, when it broke, shook the industry: the surfers' group was going to formally challenge Mavericks Surf Ventures for the right to be awarded the permit to host the contest. And when Washburn finally made public the details, the news became more astonishing still: the group had locked down Barracuda as its primary benefactor, to the tune of $500,000 per year for three years. Those calls from Perone to surfers like Skindog Collins and Shane Desmond had ultimately borne great fruit. Barracuda would look for two or three other primary sponsors to split the cost, but if none materialized, the company was willing to go it alone. Perone had loved the ethic of the event and wanted to keep it going. He told the surfers they would have veto power over any sponsorships. They would retain the vote on when to call the event itself. The decision, in the end, felt easy. Grant and his colleagues were trying to take Maverick's back to its glorious, simplified roots.

Part of that process meant that Jeff Clark had to be involved. The surfers' group reached out to Clark on the grounds that as long as Jeff was alive, it was insane, just brutally stupid, not to capitalize on his presence and his knowledge—and besides, he was one of them. If Jeff's primary objection had been Keir's involvement, then getting him aligned with the surfers ought to be no problem. It was a good thing for everybody, but especially for the surfers who loved Clark. Bringing in Jeff as a consultant to the calling of the contest was a masterstroke; it would get Clark back in the game where he belonged and it would tap his institutional memory of their beloved surf point. There was talk of a Jeff Clark celebrity golf tournament, the kind of casual-hosting thing that Jeff did so well because it played to his enthusiasms. The final decision-making process on calling the contest itself was going to remain democratized, and it therefore spread responsibility among the contestants themselves. It also made the idea feel pure, as it was the surfers doing the talking, reaching a consensus that they could live with on the contest in which they would compete. But they would have Jeff's expertise and his lifetime of experience at Mavs to draw on; Jeff would be given a voice and a platform by people who were genuinely interested in what he had to say. No one doubted that his word would carry the same weight it always had. In the water, he remained an absolute leader.

The event itself, though, would be out of Jeff's hands, organized by people like Brilhart, a longtime friend of Maverick's whose Southern California company already had successfully run several surf events in the Los Angeles area. Katherine Kelly Clark, widely appreciated and valued by the surfers for her local knowledge and ability to open doors, was going to be invited on board; the surfers decided that Jeff could either choose to deal with that or not. Frank Quirarte, a longtime photographer who was one of the last ties to Keir's company, was both wanted and wooed to the new venture.

Washburn, taking the reins, e-mailed all of the surfers the details of the proposal; the return sentiment was virtually unanimous in favor of making the break from MSV. And when Grant shared with them one of the ideas for what to call the new contest, their enthusiasm spiked anew.

His news? The event would be dubbed The Jay at Maverick's. Jay Moriarity would ride again.

In the short history of Maverick's, perhaps no surfer had ever been as universally beloved as Moriarity. He burst onto the scene at Pillar Point in 1993 as a fifteen-year-old wunderkind, and he was still a fresh-faced soul when he died at age twenty-two, the victim of a shallow-water blackout while free-diving in the Maldives, off the coast of India, in 2001. It was a death, inexplicable and wrenching, that shook the Maverick's group to its core. But in the years that followed, the conversation about Jay gradually returned its focus almost exclusively onto how he had lived.

Moriarity was a surfer well beyond his years, this partly the product of his tutelage by Santa Cruz legend Frosty Hesson. He came to Maverick's for the first time already fully steeped in the knowledge of how the wave broke, and when, and why. From the beginning, Jay surfed it well, like a grown man. He commanded almost instant respect. And he was a beautiful human, with his close-cropped hair and dazzling smile and soulful hazel eyes. The photographs of the era tended to bathe Jay in the golden hue of late afternoon sunlight. He was an almost prototypical poster boy for the sport.

But it was all the rest of Moriarity that made him memorable. Despite growing up in Santa Cruz, a place notorious for its west-side-versus-east-side surfer infighting and a general tendency toward provincialism, Jay was the ultimate open door. He had no interest in pinning anyone down to geography. All were equal when they paddled out: that was his mantra.

"The one person who cut through all the muck was Jay," Washburn said. "Jay saw the Santa Cruz east side and west side, and he's like, 'What's that? You guys have no sides.' He was a little kid at the time, but he still had the ability to see it differently. It came to me that it was just perfect—that our thing wouldn't happen without him. Like all these years after he's gone, he is still the reason that it's gonna work."

The idea of bestowing Jay's name upon the contest worked on several levels. Most obviously, it called to mind the true spirit of the event, which was a love of surfing big waves and the camaraderie that existed among the few souls who were willing to go out there and try. But bringing Moriarity into it also had a way of defining the event, as Eddie Aikau's name had done for the Waimea big-wave contest years earlier. And Jay's spirit and memory were such that they had the capacity to bring people with radically viewpoints to the same table. Mel and Washburn knew that both Katherine and Jeff Clark had been very close to Jay; perhaps by invoking Jay's name, the surfers could even get those two to find a middle ground that allowed them both to contribute.

The thing was no slam dunk, of course. Among other issues, Mavericks Surf Ventures had successfully bid for the permit from the Harbor Commission that allowed it to host the event for several years running. The application process cost $15,000, and the commission intended to issue only one permit per season. Although nothing much had been heard from MSV over the past few months, there was no doubt that

Keir would fight with everything he had to retain the permit;
it was his ultimate trump card. If MSV won it again, the surfers' only recourse would be to boycott the contest and try to
force Beadling to stand down. Surely the Harbor Commission
could see that the contest just past was a disaster in every
way except the waves; surely the commissioners knew that
Beadling had been sued by Jeff Clark. In some respects, the
surfers were counting on common sense to carry the day—but
no one underestimated Keir as a tactical opponent.

Jeff's participation in the Jay group was not assured.
Because it was Jeff, it was complicated. The surfers all wanted
him back, but Jeff still wanted to get paid, and he and the
management would have to come to some agreement on what
his presence was worth going forward. Several of his friends
quietly hoped that Jeff would see the advantage of being back
in the mix and back in his rightful place as the leading voice
at the surf point. It ought to be good for his board business, if
nothing else. But Jeff's outlook was clouded by the fact that
he was in the process of settling his lawsuit against Beadling
and MSV. It stood to reason that his settlement would be
significantly diminished if MSV had no ability to pay—that
is, if the creation of a new contest meant insolvency for Keir's
company. Even though Jeff was relinquishing all of his stock
in the company via the settlement, his payout was tied directly
to MSV still functioning on some level. Barracuda wanted the
surfers and it wanted Jeff, but it wanted Jeff at a price that
was reasonable and workable. Everybody involved felt that Jeff
would eventually do the right thing, on the right terms. It was
inconceivable that he could stay away from his own backyard.

In midsummer of 2010, the surfers publicly announced their plans. They were quickly dubbed the Jay Group by the local media, which was almost too perfect to be true: It gave them a collective image and a definition that would have been impossible to achieve otherwise. As expected, Keir began working furiously to defend his turf. He reached out to Peter Mel; he called Greg Long. He began to contact some of the younger surfers in hopes of reminding them how steadfast MSV had been in supporting the contest over the years, how diligently Beadling had worked to line up funding during lean economic times. But he was on top of a huge wave and facing a stiff offshore breeze. Keir was about to get thrown off the back side.

In August, Harbor District general manager Peter Grenell announced that he would recommend that the commissioners again grant the permit to Mavericks Surf Ventures. Within a couple of days, though, days buffeted by a flurry of complaints and a rash of new information about the Jay Group and about MSV's purported shortcomings, a planned vote on the permit issue was abruptly scrapped. The Jay Group was beginning to fire its big guns. Keir responded by highlighting his company's years of experience running a very complicated event, but as stories of delayed or missed payments began to trickle out, the situation looked worse and worse. At a public hearing related only tangentially to the issue, some sixty surfers showed up to profess their support for the Jay Group, and Washburn called out Beadling by name for his company's subpar management of the contest. "Keir hasn't done a good job," Washburn said. "MSV hasn't done right by the group, by the contest."

Keir and his company did have history with the Harbor

Commission, but it also faced this litany of complaint, and in terms of public perception MSV was on the hook for the 2010 event at which so many people on the beach had been injured. The very thing that Beadling had spent years trying to build was now threatening to collapse under its own weight. The new group had virtually every significant surfer on its side; for that matter, the surfers were saying that even if MSV were granted the permit, they would not take part in any contest that Keir fronted. They had no qualms about taking their case to the media, and the local newspapers and television stations lapped up the controversy and magnified the idea of a "true spirit" group trying to wrest control of Maverick's from the corporate world. The commission's hand was being forced, and in a very public way.

At a meeting in fall 2010, the dominoes finally fell. Armed with its new information about how the Jay Group, now dubbed HMB Surf Group, Inc., would run the event, commissioners awarded the crucial permit to the new surfers' collaborative. The surfers were now on the clock to try to produce an event of their own—and in one of their first formal acts, the organizers of the Jay at Maverick's Big Wave Invitational moved to address the chaos on the beach from the preceding February. They announced that, in consultation with the Harbor District, they would no longer allow spectators on the sand or the bluff above, an open attempt at preventing the kind of scene that had seemingly doomed Keir and MSV. Despite the inherent difficulty of deciding who could and could not have access to an ostensibly public place, the move was greeted with some enthusiasm and general support in the local media. It would be a different look, certainly. Maverick's was going all the way back to its roots: virtually unseen from shore.

Grant Washburn had become the go-to person for updates, news, and sound bites. It was, for Washburn, a full step into the spotlight that had only occasionally been trained on him in the past. Until that year, Grant was the person to whom people went with questions about the physical or spiritual qualities of Maverick's. Now they were going to be asking him about its future.

Not long thereafter, Jeff Clark announced that he had decided to officially be a part of the new venture, and that he would work the safety patrol on the contest day, back on the water where he belonged. It was the right decision, but as were most things with Clark, it was not without some friction. Clark took to the local papers to mention that he would not run the contest the way the new organizers were planning to run it, particularly the idea that the field of twenty-four surfers was determined partially on a vote and partially by dint of having placed well in the event the year before. Clark wanted every surfer to earn his way into the event. He also said that he felt it should be the prerogative of the "contest director" to call off a scheduled event if the conditions so dictated, be they too mild or too dangerous. The implication was clear enough: Clark had been the only recognized "director" in the history of the contest, whereas now it was democratized. Washburn and his fellow organizers did not respond to those words; instead, they cheerfully pointed out that virtually the entire Maverick's surf community was on board with the new model for determining the field of contestants. Anyway, they had Jeff back. Surely everyone involved could figure out how to make that work.

Keir Beadling was left with a company, an apparel line, and the trademarked rights to a contest that, as of the fall of 2010, no longer held one of the critical pieces of paper needed to operate at Pillar Point. What his company did have, Beadling asserted, was intellectual property on the event and the Mavericks Surf Contest name that made it legally difficult for anyone else to conduct an event there without running afoul of MSV's rights. In the meantime, MSV continued to market Mavericks as a brand on its web site, though there was no mention of the 2010–11 contest. What there was, on the site, was a new line of cold-weather gear, caps, hoodies, corduroy jackets, and the like, just in time for the holiday buying season.

In the end, some believed that this split, however acrimoniously achieved, might ultimately be something both parties could live with. The surfers had their contest and their turf; Beadling had an apparel and marketing business related to Maverick's, the kind of thing that might still someday realize his dream of outstripping the contest itself and simply becoming its own iconic brand. (In one of those predictable results, the official supplier of the new Jay at Maverick's contest gear would be Jeff Clark's equally new surf shop, now relocated to a prime spot in the Pillar Point Harbor dockside area.) If it didn't fly, Keir would undoubtedly compartmentalize the experience and move on to something else. He was, in the final analysis, an entrepreneur.

Near the end of November 2010, most of the new group of twenty-four contest invitees made their way to that thin strip of sand just before the jetty that led to the Maverick's surf point. They shook hands, hugged each other with the warm friendship of kindred spirits. It was about to be another big-wave season at Mavs. This time, the surfers were the ones calling the shots.

At the center of the proceedings, Jeff Clark beamed like a man who'd been granted a new lease on life. The bounce had returned to his step. Physically, Clark appeared to be fully recovered from his painful hip issues, and emotionally he was back where he needed to be, among his friends and peers, revered for his experience and knowledge and his love of the things that he truly valued. The contest window would open on December 1 and extend to the end of February. Assuming the waves showed up, the money was there. The vendors would be paid. The surfers would be paid. And the people who ran the event were going to be allowed, at least for a while, to prove their claim that it was about honoring the spirit of the place and of people like Jay Moriarity.

That window of opportunity closed faster than anyone involved could have imagined, but perhaps it was just another fitting chapter at Maverick's, a place around which no one ever appeared to settle into anything resembling comfortability. A series of incessantly flat days and weeks killed the 2010–11 contest, the entire period drifting by without the much-anticipated event being called. Not long after came the stunning news that Barracuda Networks was withdrawing as the primary sponsor, just one year into an expected three-year relationship, and that

Jay Moriarity's family also had requested his name no longer be associated with the contest. The series of developments, each of them offered with almost no explanation, left the future of the "Super Bowl of big-wave surfing" in legitimate doubt. There was no title sponsor. There was word of infighting among the would-be organizers. Grant Washburn and his colleagues geared up for another attempt to secure financing. Clark, moving in from the periphery, mentioned in an interview that he would like to take over the event. Keir Beadling's claim to intellectual property had yet to be fully addressed. Maverick's, once again, had roared into a full upheaval.

But of course all of that was about the business, about the contest. Viewed from certain angles, it was only about what happened one day out of the year. For those who had really come to know the site, Maverick's didn't function like that at all. In fact, Mavs was often at its best when nobody was looking.

Some of the people who had been there the longest told the story of a late evening in 2001, when Jay Moriarity and Jeff Clark took to the water together and traded incredible rides, one after the other, with almost no one else around. There were no cameras. No one asked for an interview afterward. It was simply an older salt and a younger buck meeting as equals on the wave, kicking it up and enjoying the force in relative peace and quiet. As Clark later remembered the story, the two of them needed the lights of the harbor to provide their bearing and guide them home as they paddled back in amid the gathering darkness. It was still and calm as they finally walked out of the water and onto the sand. It was a few months before Jay died.

Grant Washburn believed that Jay's spirit infused the place still, as did the spirit of so many of the great surfers who had come through. The spirit kept drawing them; that much seemed obvious. But of course the big-wave riders were moved to gather wherever and whenever they could anyway, all in the name of chasing that high on the water. Not long after he returned from the expedited and costly trip to Todos Santos, a weekend in which he failed to make it out of the first round, Chris Bertish fired off an e-mail to his big-wave colleagues laying out a review of his itinerary that weekend: thirty-four hours out and forty-two hours against the time change back to South Africa, arriving at the far end of the weekend with only an hour before he was to begin making business calls on clients.

"All this," Chris wrote, "at a cost of borrowing another 25,000 rand from my brother—over $3,000. Was it worth it? . . . For frikken sure, without a doubt in my mind. To drop everything, fly halfway around the world to go and surf some of the best big waves in the world with friends and heroes, and just to see the look of pure stoke, joy and celebration on Mark Healy's well-deserved face when he got announced the winner . . . I would have dropped double the amount without blinking an eye."

It was pure Bertish, the note; he had been proving his love for and commitment to the waves for years. But he would no longer need to borrow that money. In August, the international surf brand O'Neill announced that it had signed Chris as its premier big-wave rider. The sponsorship deal would essentially finance all of Bertish's competitions around the globe.

That list, forevermore, would include Maverick's. Chris now planned to return again and again to the place he had fallen in love with, the one that he spent so many years trying to find a way inside. Jeff had finally given him that chance, and Chris had made the most of it, just as Twiggy had done in 2006, when he came blasting out of nowhere to win it all. The big waves were like that. On any given day, they were the province of the rider who stood up the tallest and was the most willing to make the drop, and personal history was about the farthest point removed from relevance. It was how Flea had won those first three go-rounds; it was certainly how Chris had won on the biggest paddle-in day in history. And it meant that Jeff had been right again. It meant that Jeff knew what he was doing when he found a place for Bertish two years before.

It always came back to Jeff, anyway. Every conversation about Maverick's referenced him in some way or another. The surf point was his in all of the important ways, none of which you could take to the bank and cash. Jeff still knew it better than anyone alive. He understood how the wave could surprise you, how it could take a sinister turn, how a shift in the tides could rearrange everything about your ride. He was an astute observer of the conditions because he had been observing them for most of his waking life.

Toby Garfield, the oceanographer at San Francisco State, didn't balk when it was suggested to him that people like Clark were really talking science when they talked about the wave and how it might be acting on any given day. "Surfers to me are a lot like fishermen," Garfield said, "in that they're out there all the time, observing it. They can't help but figure it out. If you want to know a lot about the weather and coastal conditions, go talk to a fisherman. It's the same with the surfers. The serious ones understand—they'll pick it up pretty quick."

Several months after Garfield spoke those words, two incidents at Maverick's thrust the place violently back into the public eye. In January 2011, a thirty-year-old Southern California surfer named Jacob Trette found himself caught at the very top of a massive barrel at Mavs, hurled over the falls, buried deep in the frigid water, and knocked out by one of the ensuing waves that landed on his head. Saved by another sled rescue, found floating face-down in the shallows, Trette would be placed in a medically induced coma for two days before eventually making a full recovery. His near fatality occurred on the second day he had ever surfed the point.

"Just a face full of water, that's all I remember," Trette later told NBC *Today Show* host Matt Lauer, as news of the man's rescue—by a photographer, Russell Ord, who happened to be in the channel on a banned Jet Ski and raced in to drag the unconscious surfer to safety—blew up nationally. "It was like Mother Nature gave me a right cross, like Mike Tyson punched me in the face."

Trette spoke as a survivor whose rapid recovery stunned even those attending him at the hospital. Less than two months later, there would be no such miraculous turn of events. Maverick's was reclaiming its turf, and it was taking a victim in the process.

On March 16, 2011, near six o'clock in the evening, a Hawaiian surfer named Sion Milosky paddled into a monster break just off Pillar Point. It was the far side of a nearly perfect day of big-wave riding, one that many of the locals would later recall as a classic Mavs session. Wave faces were opening up to 40 and 45 feet. The point was attended by many of the elite surfers in Maverick's history. Jeff Clark was there. Kenny "Skindog" Collins, who had hosted Milosky at his west side Santa Cruz home the previous four days, was on the water. Grant Washburn was there, and Nathan Fletcher, and Shawn Dollar, the young charger who had pushed the limits of the sport by surfing that mammoth wave just before the finals session on contest day the year before.

Milosky was a thirty-five-year-old welder who had recently been named Hawaii's North Shore Underground Surfer of the Year, an honor bestowed in acknowledgment of a hardcore group of publicity-shunning locals there who surfed strictly for the pleasure of being on the water and the thrill of the chase. He was regarded as a first-rate big-wave surfer, and although the week marked only his second foray to Half Moon Bay, he already was riding Maverick's like a veteran. On the day of the sixteenth, Milosky was preparing to stand up on what observers guessed was his sixth huge wave of the session. It was in an especially dangerous takeoff area, one farther out to sea than normal; that was where the huge breakers were rolling. The big riders chased the big waves.

As Milosky got to his feet and began to fire down the face of the wave, its lip took a sudden and violent lurch over the top. It was as though the wave literally changed configuration in the middle of its break. The lip quickly closed down hard on Milosky, hammering him below the water's surface. A surf filmmaker named Chris Killen, positioned just off the side of the wave on a Jet Ski, later told the *Santa Cruz Sentinel*, "He was really deep and he makes the drop, and the end section comes and just explodes behind him as he straightens out." It was the last time anyone saw Milosky alive; though his surf-board was seen tombstoning in the water a few minutes later, his body was not discovered until twenty minutes after that by Nathan Fletcher, near the entrance to Pillar Point Harbor. It was a drowning. Those who saw Milosky's body as he was laid down on dry land said there appeared to be not a mark on him. Milosky was married and the father of two young children.

Though Killen and another surf photographer tried in vain to find Milosky with their Jet Skis, Jacob Trette was essentially saved by Russell Ord's quick action on his personal watercraft, a development that gave people like Jeff Clark another reason to believe it essential that PWCs be allowed in the surf area at all times. But Trette's misfortune and Milosky's death under-score a more basic truth about Maverick's: even in an age of comparative notoriety and renown, the wave remains elusive and hostile to even the most experienced and dedicated riders, particularly if what they lack is a longtime working knowledge of the surf point itself. For most of the regulars, the veteran core, the opportunity to get to know Maverick's might very well become a lifetime pursuit.

In San Francisco there existed a public presentation called *Ask a Scientist*, an evening panel, café-talk-style program. Once, Toby Garfield was invited to talk about the science of big waves, and the moderator invited Grant Washburn to come along and provide the surfers' perspective. "I probably got more out of the evening than Grant did," Garfield said.

"It was so much fun. His way of explaining it and my way of explaining it were basically the same—I just knew some of the technical terms. But these guys really get it."

Washburn had learned from Jeff, and then learned and relearned for himself, the point of respecting the wave without bowing to it. The fun of getting on the board, after all, was in seeing what it could do, and that often meant reaching for the next level of accomplishment even if no one but the other surfers would ever understand what you had already achieved. "Nobody else gets it anyway," Washburn said. "You're really impressing the guys who know a difference between 25 feet and 26 feet, which is a huge difference when you're out on a wave like that. It comes out of that deep water, and it's several blocks wide, and then it hits this shallow thing and comes to a height—but height isn't the right measure. It's the energy sphere of that wave, just a gargantuan thing. And who can understand that from anywhere besides the wave? It's personal."

It was personal; it was historic; it was poetic; it was epic. The wave was the thing. Up on Avenue Balboa, looking out from his deck, Jeff Clark talked to a visitor one morning without ever really taking his eye off the surf point. It was beautiful and furious, even from far away, and Clark could tell with a glance whether the day had a chance to be special.

"I think I'm gonna head down and check it out," he said suddenly, lifting himself out of the deck chair in a single, powerful motion. Clark fairly bounded across the carpeted living room. He seemed in a sudden hurry. Maverick's, once again, was waiting.

ACKNOWLEDGMENTS

The idea of an Oklahoman writing a book having anything to do with surfing certainly ought to be understood as the most drastic long shot on the board. I am indebted to several people for bringing that project home.

My brilliant editor at Norton, Brendan Curry, guided this book from vaguely exotic idea to finished product with a consistency of optimistic calm that would be difficult to overstate. I owe him tremendously. Many thanks as well to my friend and agent Bob Mecoy, who found the perfect home for this project during turbulent times.

Much gratitude to the redoubtable Nancy Palmquist and Melanie Tortoroli at Norton, as well as to Renee Schwartz for her thoughtful reading of the manuscript. Allegra Huston contributed critical and careful copyediting. From start to finish, working with everyone associated with Norton has been an absolute pleasure and a writer's dream.

My ability to report and write *The Voodoo Wave* was dependent on the willingness of those who have lived the Maverick's story to share it with me. I hope the book is equal to their generosity, which was far and wide. Very special thanks in particular to Chris Bertish, Grant "Twiggy" Baker, Randy Cone, the great Bruce Jenkins, Grant Washburn, and Keir Beadling. Washburn and Beadling each sat through multiple interviews with remarkable composure, even as the world of Maverick's around them changed radically.

Though I drew much of Chris Bertish's story from his direct interviews with me, I gained wonderful insight and detail through his web site, www.chrisbertish.com, which I recommend to anyone who would like to read further. I would also like to suggest the books *Inside Maverick's: Portrait of a Monster Wave* and *Maverick's: The Story of Big-Wave Surfing*, both indispensable to those who would understand the goings-on around Pillar Point. My deep thanks to the surf writers and photographers who shared their knowledge and enthusiasm along the way.

I wrote the many drafts of this book while also contributing columns to ESPN.com under the guidance of Michael Knisley, a good friend and a great editor. And I am sincerely grateful to Steve Cottingim and the people at radio station KHTK in Sacramento, CA, where I have been fortunate enough to be part of the on-air staff for the past couple of years. A special shout-out to Kevin Gleason, Mark Lowe, Joe Pittman, and Dave Mason for their support.

Ongoing love to Rachel and Fitz; my brother, Steve; my sister, Kay; and their fabulous families. Thanks to Jim, Mitch,

Kevin, and Blake for the laughs, coming soon to a ballpark near you. Appreciation to Tim Flannery for once upon a time explaining to me the basics of surfing, never dreaming that I would someday commit the offense of attempting a book about the subject.

To Jim and Lori McElligott: This simple thank-you would never cover it, but it'll have to do. We look forward to every visit with you, Cody, Dylan, Bud, and Beverly, and every visit is too brief.

My life is full because of the people with whom I share it. Love to my massive extended family and to my sons, Pat and Ryan, who might yet become soul surfers. My beautiful, long-suffering wife, Colleen, an editor to her core, has endured thorough readings of every draft of every book I've written. She has my sympathy, my heart, and 50 percent responsibility for the bills.

ABOUT THE AUTHOR

MARK KREIDLER is the author of *Four Days to Glory: Wrestling with the Soul of the American Heartland* and *Six Good Innings: How One Small Town Became a Little League Giant*, and is a regular contributor to ESPN.com and CBS radio. He lives in Northern California with his wife and sons.